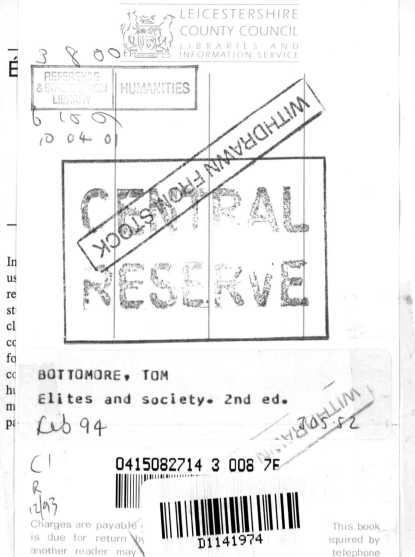

Élites and society

Second edition

Tom Bottomore

London and New York

First published 1964 by C.A. Watts

Second edition published 1993
by Routledge
11 New Fetter Lane, London EC4P 4EE

Simultaneously published in the USA and Canada
by Routledge
29 West 35th Street, New York, NY 10001

Typeset in Times by
NWL Editorial Services, Langport, Somerset
Printed and bound in Great Britain by
T.J. Press (Padstow) Ltd, Padstow, Cornwall

British Library Cataloguing in Publication Data
A catalogue record for this book is available from the British
Library.

Library of Congress Cataloging in Publication Data
Bottomore, T.B. – 2nd ed.
  Élites and society: Second edition / Tom Bottomore
  p. cm.
  Includes bibliographical references and index.
  1. Elite (Social sciences) 2. Leadership. 3. Class distinction.
  I. Title.
  HM141.B824   1993   92–38181
  305.5′2 – dc20   CIP

ISBN 0–415–08271–4 (pbk)

Contents

1 The élite: concept and ideology   1

2 From the ruling class to the power élite   15

3 Politics and the circulation of élites   35

4 Intellectuals, managers and bureaucrats   52

**5 Tradition and modernity: élites in the developing
countries**   72

6 Democracy and the plurality of élites   87

7 Equality or élites?   101

8 Into the millennium   119

Bibliography   132
Name index   138
Subject index   140

Chapter 1

The élite
Concept and ideology

The word '*élite*' was used in the seventeenth century to describe commodities of particular excellence; and the usage was later extended to refer to superior social groups, such as prestigious military units or the higher ranks of the nobility.[1] In the English language the earliest known use of 'élite', according to the *Oxford English Dictionary*, is in 1823, at which time it was already applied to social groups. But the term did not become widely used in social and political writing until late in the nineteenth century in Europe, or until the 1930s in Britain and America, when it was diffused through the sociological theories of élites, notably in the writings of Vilfredo Pareto.

In his *Treatise on General Sociology* (1915–19) Pareto defined 'élite' in two different ways. He began with a very general definition:

> Let us assume that in every branch of human activity each individual is given an index which stands as a sign of his capacity, very much the way grades are given in the various subjects in examinations in school. The highest type of lawyer, for instance, will be given 10. The man who does not get a client will be given 1 – reserving zero for the man who is an out-and-out idiot. To the man who has made his millions – honestly or dishonestly as the case may be – we will give 10. To the man who has earned his thousands we will give 6; to such as just manage to keep out of the poor-house 1, keeping zero for those who get in . . . And so on for all the branches of human activity . . . So let us make a class of the people who have the highest indices in their branch of activity, and to that class give the name of élite.

> (pp. 1422–3)

Pareto himself does not make any further use of this concept of élite; it serves merely to emphasize the inequality of individual endowment in every sphere of social life, and as the starting point for a definition of the 'governing élite', which is his real subject matter.

> For the particular investigation with which we are engaged, a study of the social equilibrium, it will help if we further divide that class [the élite] into two classes: a *governing élite*, comprising individuals who directly or indirectly play some considerable part in government, and a *non-governing élite*, comprising the rest . . . So we get two strata in a population: (1) A lower stratum, the *non-élite*, with whose possible influence on government we are not just here concerned; then (2) a higher stratum, the *élite*, which is divided into two: (a) a governing *élite*; (b) a non-governing *élite*.

> (pp. 1423–4)

It is not difficult to discover, from Pareto's earlier writings, how he arrived at this conception. In his *Cours d'économie politique* (1896–7) he had propounded the idea of a normal curve of the distribution of wealth in a society. In *Les systèmes socialistes* (1902) he went on to argue, first, that if individuals were arranged according to other criteria, such as their level of intelligence, aptitude for mathematics, musical talent, moral character, etc., there would probably result distribution curves similar to that for wealth; and secondly, that if individuals were arranged according to their degree of political and social power or influence, it would be found in most societies that the same individuals occupied the same place in this hierarchy as in the hierarchy of wealth. 'The so-called upper classes are also usually the richest. These classes represent an élite, an "aristocracy" ' (vol. I, p. 28).

Nevertheless, there is an important difference in the formulation of the question in his *Treatise*, for Pareto here concerns himself not with a curve of distribution of certain attributes (including power and influence), but with a simple opposition between those who have power, the 'governing élite', and those who have none, the masses. This change in Pareto's conception may well have owed something to the work of Gaetano Mosca, who was the first to make a systematic distinction between 'élite' and masses – though using other terms – and to attempt the construction of a new science of politics on this foundation. Mosca expressed his fundamental idea in these words:

> Among the constant facts and tendencies that are to be found in all political organisms, one is so obvious that it is apparent to the most casual eye. In all societies – from societies that are very meagrely developed and have barely attained the dawnings of civilization, down to the most advanced and powerful societies – two classes of people appear – a class that rules and a class that is ruled. The first class, always the less numerous, performs all political functions, monopolizes power and enjoys the advantages that power brings, whereas the second, the more numerous class, is directed and controlled by the first, in a manner that is now more or less legal, now more or less arbitrary and violent.[2]

> (1939, p. 50)

Mosca explains the rule of the minority over the majority by the fact that the former is organized –

> the dominion of an organized minority, obeying a single impulse, over the unorganized majority is inevitable. The power of any minority is irresistible as against each single individual in the majority, who stands alone before the totality of the organized minority. At the same time, the minority is organized for the very reason that it is a minority.

– and also by the fact that the minority is usually composed of superior individuals –

> members of a ruling minority regularly have some attribute, real or apparent, which is highly esteemed and very influential in the society in which they live.

> (1939, p. 53)

Both Mosca and Pareto, therefore, were concerned with élites in the sense of groups of people who either exercised directly, or were in a position to influence very strongly the exercise of, political power. At the same time, they recognized that the 'governing élite' or 'political class' is itself composed of distinct social groups. Pareto (1915–19, pp. 1429–30) observed that the 'upper stratum of society, the élite, nominally contains certain groups of people, not always very sharply defined, that are called aristocracies', and he went on to refer to 'military, religious, and commercial aristocracies and plutocracies'. The point was made more sharply in a study of élites in France by a pupil of Pareto, Marie Kolabinska (1912), who discussed explicitly the movement of individuals between the different sub-groups of the governing élite, and set out to examine in some detail the history of four such groups: the rich, the nobles, the armed aristocracy and the clergy. Nevertheless, Pareto is always inclined to emphasize more strongly the division between the governing élite and the non-élite, and it is Mosca who examines more thoroughly the composition of the élite itself, especially in the modern democratic societies. Thus he refers to 'the various party organizations into which the political class is divided'(1939, p. 411), and which have to compete for the votes of the more numerous classes; and later on he remarks that

> it cannot be denied that the representative system [of government] provides a way for many different social forces to participate in the political system and, therefore, to balance and limit the influence of other social forces and the influence of bureaucracy in particular.

> (ibid., p. 258)

This last passage also reveals a considerable divergence between Pareto and Mosca in their interpretation of the development of political systems. Pareto always emphasizes the universality of the distinction between governing élite and masses, and he reserves his most scathing comments for the modern notions of 'democracy', 'humanitarianism' and 'progress'. Mosca, on the other hand, is prepared to recognize, and in a qualified way to approve, the distinctive features of modern democracy. In his first book (1884), it is true, he observes that in a parliamentary democracy, 'the representative is not elected by the voters but, as a rule, has himself elected by them . . . or . . . his friends have him elected' (pp. 250–1); but in his later works he concedes that the majority may, through its representatives, have a certain control over government policy. As Meisel (1958) notes, it is only in his criticism of Marx that Mosca makes a sharp disjunction between masses and minorities; for the most part he presents a more subtle and complex theory in which the political class itself is influenced and restrained by a variety of 'social forces' (representing numerous different interests in society), and also by the moral unity of the society as a whole which is expressed in the rule of law. In Mosca's theory, an élite does not simply rule by force and fraud, but 'represents', in some sense, the interests and purposes of important and influential groups in the society.

There is another element, too, in Mosca's theory which modifies its original stark outlines. In modern times, the élite is not simply raised high above the rest of society; it is intimately connected with society through a sub-élite, a much larger group which comprises, to all intents and purposes, the whole 'new middle class' of civil servants, managers and white-collar workers, scientists and engineers, scholars and intellectuals. This group does not only supply recruits to the élite (the ruling class in the narrow sense); it is itself a vital element in the government of society, and Mosca observes that 'the stability of any political organism depends on the level of morality, intelligence and activity that this second stratum has attained' (1939, p. 404). It is not unreasonable, then, to claim, as did Gramsci (1964a), that Mosca's

> political class . . . is a puzzle. One does not exactly understand what Mosca means, so fluctuating and elastic is the notion. Sometimes he seems to think of the middle class, sometimes of men of property in general, and then again of those who call themselves 'the educated'. But on other occasions Mosca apparently has in mind the 'political personnel'.
>
> (p. 140)

And later, with more certainty:

> Mosca's 'political class' is nothing but the intellectual section of the ruling group. Mosca's term approximates Pareto's élite concept – another attempt to interpret the historical phenomenon of the intelligentsia and its function in political and social life.[3]
>
> (Gramsci 1964b, p. 4 n1)

The conceptual scheme which Mosca and Pareto have handed down thus comprises the following common notions: in every society there is, and must be, a minority which rules over the rest of society; this minority – the 'political class' or 'governing élite', composed of those who occupy the posts of political command and, more vaguely, those who can directly influence political decisions – undergoes changes in its membership over a period of time, ordinarily by the recruitment of new individual members from the lower strata of society, sometimes by the incorporation of new social groups, and occasionally by the complete replacement of the established élite by a 'counter-élite', as occurs in revolutions. This phenomenon, the 'circulation of élites', will be examined more fully in a later chapter. From this point, the conceptions of Pareto and Mosca diverge. Pareto insists more strongly upon the separation between rulers and ruled in every society, and dismisses the view that a democratic political system differs from any other in this respect.[4] He explains the circulation of élites in mainly psychological terms, making use of the idea of residues (sentiments) which he set out at great length in the earlier parts of his *Treatise* (1915–19, chaps 6–8). Mosca, on the other hand, is much more aware of the heterogeneity of the élite, the higher stratum of the political class, itself; of the interests or social forces which are represented in it; and, in the case of modern societies, of its intimate bonds with the rest of society, principally through the lower stratum of the political class, the 'new middle class'. Thus Mosca also allows that there is a difference between modern democracies and other types of polity, and to some extent he recognizes that there is interaction between the ruling minority and the majority, instead of a simple dominance by the former over the latter. Finally, Mosca explains the circulation of élites sociologically as well as psychologically, insofar as he accounts for the rise of new élites (or of new elements in the élite) in part by the emergence of social forces which represent new interests (be they technological, economic, or cultural) in the society.[5]

Many later studies of élites followed Pareto and Mosca, especially the latter, closely in their concern with problems of political power. Thus H.D. Lasswell, both in his early writings, which were commended by Mosca himself, and later in the Hoover Institute Studies on élites, devoted himself particularly to the study of the political élite, which he defined in the following terms: 'The political élite comprises the power holders of a body politic. The power holders include the leadership and the social formations from which leaders typically come, and to which accountability is maintained, during a given period' (Lasswell *et al.*, 1952). The difference from the conceptions of Pareto and Mosca is that the political élite is here distinguished from other élites which are less closely associated with the exercise of power, although they may have a considerable social influence, and that the idea of 'social formations' (including social classes) from which élites are typically recruited is re-introduced into a scheme of thought from which, especially in Pareto's theory, it had been expelled. A similar development is apparent in the writings of Raymond Aron (1950, 1960), who was also chiefly concerned with the élite in the sense of a governing minority, but attempted to establish a relation between the élite and social classes,[6] at the same time emphasizing the plurality of élites in modern societies and examining the social influence of the intellectual élite, which does not ordinarily form part of the system of political power (Aron 1957).

The fresh distinctions and refinements which have been made in the concept of the élite call for a more discriminating terminology than has been employed hitherto.[7] The term 'élite (s)' is now generally applied, in fact, to functional, mainly occupational, groups which have high status (for whatever reason) in a society; and I shall use it, though with some later qualifications, in this sense. The study of such élites may be fruitful in several ways: the size of the élites, the number of different élites, their relations with each other and with the groups that wield political power, are among the important facts which have to be considered in distinguishing between different types of society and in accounting for changes in social structure; so, too, is the closed or open character of the élites, or in other words, the nature of the recruitment of their members and the degree of social mobility which this implies. If the general term 'élite' is to be applied to these functional groups, we shall need another term for the minority which rules a society, which is not a functional group in the same sense, and is in any case of such great social importance that it deserves to be given a distinctive name. I shall use here Mosca's term, the 'political class', to refer to all those groups which exercise political power or influence, and are directly engaged in struggles for political leadership; and I shall distinguish within the political class a smaller group, the political élite, or governing élite, which comprises those individuals who actually exercise political power in a society at any given time. The extent of the political élite is, therefore, relatively easy to determine: it will include members of the government and of the high administration, military leaders, and, in some cases, politically influential families of an aristocracy or royal house and leaders of powerful economic enterprises. It is less easy to set the boundaries of the political class; it will, of course, include the political élite, but it may also include 'counter-élites' comprising the leaders of political parties which are out of office, and representatives of new social interests or classes such as trade union leaders, as well as groups of businessmen, and intellectuals who are active in politics. The political class, therefore, is composed of a number of groups which may be engaged in varying degrees of cooperation, competition or conflict with each other.

The concept of the political élite was presented by Mosca and Pareto as a key term in a new social science,[8] but it had another aspect which is scarcely less apparent in their writings: namely, that it formed part of a political doctrine which was opposed to, or critical of, modern democracy, and still more opposed to modern socialism.[9] C.J. Friedrich (1950) drew attention to the fact that the nineteenth-century European doctrines of rule by an élite of superior individuals – doctrines which encompassed Carlyle's philosophy of the hero and Nietzsche's vision of the superman as well as the more prosaic studies of Mosca, Pareto and Burckhardt – were 'all offspring of a society containing as yet many feudal remnants', and that these doctrines represented so many different attempts to revive ancient ideas of social hierarchy and to erect obstacles to the spread of democratic notions. The social environment of such doctrines was defined still more narrowly by Lukács (1954), who argued that the problem of political leadership was raised by sociologists precisely in those countries which had not succeeded in establishing a genuine bourgeois democracy, and where feudal elements were especially strong; and he pointed to Max Weber's concept of 'charisma' (in Germany) and Pareto's concept of 'élites' (in Italy) as similar and typical manifestations of this preoccupation.

The opposition between the idea of élites and the idea of democracy may be expressed in two forms: first, that the insistence in the élite theories upon the inequality of individual endowment runs counter to a fundamental strand in democratic political thought, which is inclined rather to emphasize an underlying equality of individuals; and secondly, that the notion of a governing minority contradicts the democratic theory of majority rule. But this opposition need not be by any means so rigorous and extreme as appears at first sight. If democracy is regarded as being primarily a political system, it may well be argued, as many have done, that 'government *by* the people' (i.e. the effective rule of the majority) is impossible in practice, and that the significance of political democracy is primarily that the positions of power in society are open in principle to everyone, that there is competition for power, and that the holders of power at any time are accountable to the electorate. Schumpeter (1942), following Max Weber, presented such a view of democracy, which has since been widely accepted, when he defined the democratic method as 'that institutional arrangement for arriving at political decisions in which individuals acquire the power to decide by means of a competitive struggle for the people's vote'. Similarly, Karl Mannheim, who at an earlier stage had seen in the views of the élite theorists an irrational justification of 'direct action', and of unconditional subordination to a leader, came later to regard such theories as being compatible with democracy:

> the actual shaping of policy is in the hands of élites; but this does not mean to say that the society is not democratic. For it is sufficient for democracy that the individual citizens, though prevented from taking a direct part in government all the time, have at least the possibility of making their aspirations felt at certain intervals.
>
> (1956, part III, p. 179)

Moreover, it can equally well be argued that, even if democracy is regarded as comprising more than a political system, it is still compatible with élite theories; for the idea of equality which democracy as a form of society may be held to imply can easily be reinterpreted as 'equality of opportunity'. Democracy will then be treated as a type of society in which the élites – economic and cultural, as well as political – are 'open' in principle, and are in fact recruited from different social strata on the basis of individual merit. This conception of the place of élites in a democracy is actually suggested by the theory of the circulation of élites, and is stated explicitly in Mosca's writings.

It needs to be emphasized at this point that both the conceptions I have discussed – that of political competition, and that of equality of opportunity – can be presented as corollaries of liberal, or *laissez-faire*, economic theory, as Schumpeter was quite aware: 'This concept [of competition for political leadership] presents similar difficulties as the concept of competition in the economic sphere, with which it may be usefully compared' (1942, p. 271). A later writer (Williams 1958) stated the connexion still more forcefully: 'the theory of élites is, essentially, only a refinement of social *laissez-faire*. The doctrine of opportunity in education is a mere silhouette of the doctrine of economic individualism, with its emphasis on competition and "getting- on" '(p. 236). In one sense, therefore, the élite theories of Pareto and Mosca were not (and those of their successors are not now) opposed to the general idea of democracy. Their original and main antagonist was, in fact, socialism, and especially Marxist socialism. As Mosca (1939, p. 327) wrote: 'In the world in which we are living socialism will be arrested only if a realistic political science succeeds in demolishing the metaphysical and optimistic methods that prevail at present in social studies.' This 'realistic science', which Pareto, Weber, Michels and others in different ways helped to further, was intended above all to refute Marx's theory of social classes on two essential points: first, to show that the Marxist conception of a 'ruling *class*' is erroneous, by demonstrating the continual circulation of élites, which prevents in most societies, and especially in the modern industrial societies, the formation of a stable and closed ruling class; and secondly, to show that a classless society is impossible, since in every society there is, and must be, a minority which actually rules. As Meisel (1958, p. 10) so aptly comments:

> 'Élite' was originally a middle class notion . . . [In the Marxist theory] the proletariat is to be the ultimate class which will usher in the classless society. Not so. Rather, the history of all societies, past and future, is the history of its ruling classes . . . there will always be a ruling class, and therefore exploitation. This is the anti-socialist, specifically anti-Marxist, bent of the élitist theory as it unfolds in the last decade of the nineteenth century.

The élitist theories also opposed socialist doctrines in a more general way, by substituting for the notion of a class which rules by virtue of economic or military power the notion of an élite which rules because of the superior qualities of its members. As Kolabinska (1912, p. 5) says, 'the principal notion conveyed by the term 'élite' is that of superiority'.[10]

These reflections upon the ideological elements in élite theories provoke some further questions. It is possible, as I have suggested, to reconcile the idea of élites with democratic social theories; yet the early exponents of élite theories were for the most part critical of, or hostile to, democracy (although Mosca changed his views somewhat after his experience of Fascist rule in Italy, and became a cautious defender of some aspects of democratic government), and the hostility is still more marked in the case of those, such as Carlyle and Nietzsche, who presented social myths rather than scientific theories of politics. How is this to be explained? There is, first, the fact that these nineteenth-century thinkers conceived democracy in a different way, as a stage in the 'revolt of the masses' leading with apparent necessity towards socialism. In criticizing democracy, therefore, they were, in an indirect way, combating socialism itself. It should be noticed, further, that the élite theorists themselves have had an important influence in producing the new definitions of democracy, such as that of Schumpeter, which are then held up as being compatible with the notion of élites. These developments in social thought, which have affected our modern conceptions of both democracy and socialism, will be examined more closely in a later chapter.

Another characteristic of the élite theories has been reproduced in many recent social theories which are directed against socialism; it is that, while these theories criticize the determinism which they find especially in Marxism, they themselves tend to establish an equally strict kind of determinism. The fundamental argument of the élite theorists is not merely that every known society has been divided into two strata – a ruling minority and a majority which is ruled – but that all societies must be so divided. In what respect, we may ask, is this less deterministic than Marxism? For whether human beings are obliged to attain the classless society or are necessarily prevented from ever attaining it, are they not equally unfree? It may be objected that the cases are not alike: that the élite theorists are only excluding one form of society as impossible while leaving open other possibilities (and Mosca claimed that in the social sciences it is easier to foresee *what is never going to happen* than to foresee exactly what will happen); whereas the Marxists are predicting that a particular form of society will necessarily come into existence. But one might equally well say that the élite theorists – and especially Pareto – are claiming that one type of political society is universal and necessary, and that the Marxists deny the universal validity of this 'law of élites and masses' and assert the liberty of human beings to imagine and create new forms of society. In short, there is in both theories an element of social determinism which may be more or less strongly emphasized.

I mention this question now only in order to bring out the connexion between the ideological and the theoretical aspects of the concept of élites. The concept refers to an observable social phenomenon and takes its place in theories which attempt to explain social happenings, especially political changes. At the same time the concept made its appearance in social thought at a time and in circumstances which at once gave it an ideological significance in the contest between capitalism and socialism, and it spread widely in doctrines which have an avowed ideological purpose. Even later, even in our supposedly post-ideological age, the concept cannot be regarded as a purely scientific construct; for every sociological concept and theory has an ideological force by reason of its influence upon the thoughts and actions of human beings in their everyday life. It may have this influence either because it is impregnated with a social doctrine, or because, while excluding any immediate doctrinal influence, it nevertheless draws attention to and emphasizes certain features of social life and neglects others, and thus persuades individuals to conceive of their condition and their possible future in one set of terms rather than another. To criticize a conceptual scheme or a theory in its ideological aspect is not, therefore, simply to show its connexion with a broader doctrine of human nature and society and to oppose another social doctrine to it; it is also, or mainly, to show the scientific limitations of the concepts and theories, and to propose new concepts and theories which are truer or more adequate to describe and analyse what actually occurs in social life. In what follows I shall be concerned, for the most part, with just such a critical examination of the idea of élites, and only at the end of the book shall I return to a discussion of the rival social doctrines which are powerfully if incompletely expressed through the scientific theories.

NOTES

1 See the *Dictionnaire de Trévous* (1771) where the primary meaning of *élite* is given as '*Ce qu'il y a de meilleur dans chaque espèce de marchandise*'; and it is then added that '*ce terme a passé de la boutique des marchands à d'autres usages ... (troupes d'élite, l'élite de la noblesse)*'. (Quoted in Sereno, 1938, p. 515.) In the sixteenth century, according to Edmond Huguet, *Dictionnaire de la langue française du seizième siècle*, the word *élite* meant simply *choix* (a choice); *faire élite* meant 'to make a choice'. See also, on the early uses of the term itself and of the idea of élites, Dreitzel (1962) and

Lasswell *et al.* (1952). The idea that the community should be ruled by a group of superior individuals figures prominently in Plato's thought, and even more in the Brahminical caste-doctrines which regulated ancient Indian society. In another form, which yet has an important influence upon social theories, many religious creeds have expressed the notion of an élite in terms of the 'elect of God'. The modern, social and political, conception of élites may perhaps be traced back to Saint-Simon's advocacy of the rule of scientists and industrialists; but in Saint-Simon's work the idea is qualified in numerous ways, and especially by his recognition of class differences and of the opposition between the rich and the poor, which allowed his immediate followers to develop his thought in the direction of socialism. It was in the positive philosophy of Auguste Comte that the élitist and authoritarian elements in Saint-Simon's thought, allied with the ideas of de Bonald, were restored to prominence, and so influenced directly the creators of the modern theory of élites, Mosca and Pareto.

2 This English version, *The Ruling Class*, edited by Arthur Livingston, is a conflation and rearrangement of chapters from two separate editions of Mosca's *Elementi di scienza politica* (1st edn 1896, 2nd revised and enlarged edn 1923). A study of Mosca's work by Meisel (1958) makes clear that Mosca had formulated the main elements of his doctrine in his first book, *Sulla Teorica dei governi e sul governo parlamentare: Studi storici e sociali* (1884), and shows how this doctrine was elaborated and qualified in his later writings. Meisel also discusses with great fairness (1958, chap. 8) the relation between the ideas of Mosca and Pareto and shows that the latter can hardly be convicted of simple plagiarism (as Mosca claimed); nevertheless, Pareto's later account of the governing élite does seem to owe a great deal to Mosca's doctrine. See also the recent comprehensive study of Mosca's conception of the 'political class' by Albertoni (1987).

3 See, however, the comments by Albertoni (1987, pp. 34–6), who argues that Mosca's conception had, in the context of its time, a substantial coherence, even though it combined scientific elements with ideological motives; and that it can become 'a powerful instrument for completing the Marxist interpretation of political struggle, institutions and history'.

4 Except that under the influence of democratic sentiments the governing élite is likely to be hesitant and incompetent in its rule. As so often, there is a conflict here between Pareto's science and his political doctrine; in a democratic system there is still, inevitably, a governing élite, and yet Pareto inveighs against democracy as though it were actually a real threat to the existence of such an élite.

5 Cf. Meisel, (1958, p. 303):

   like the Marxian classes, Mosca's social forces closely reflect all the changes, economic, social, cultural, of an evolving civilization. With every new need, new social forces rise to meet the challenge and to ask their share of power of the old established interests.

6 'The problem of combining in a synthesis "class" sociology and "élite" sociology . . . can be reduced to the following question: "What is the relation between social differentiation and political hierarchy in modern societies?" ' (Aron 1950, p. 128).

7 This was also proposed by Aron (1960), and I follow his suggestions to some extent.

8 Both writers insisted strongly upon the positive, scientific character of their studies, and their merits in this respect were very favourably assessed in James Burnham's *The Machiavellians* (1943).

9 The critique of socialist doctrines and movements is a prominent feature of Robert Michels' *Political Parties* (1911), which will be examined later. See also, on Michels, Beetham (1981) and Brym (1980).

10 S.F. Nadel (1956) also emphasized 'social superiority' as the distinguishing feature of an élite, without noticing the ideological element in this conception.

Chapter 2

From the ruling class to the power élite

The concern which Mosca and Pareto displayed to create a new science of politics was provoked, as we have seen, by their opposition to socialism, and especially to Marx's social theory, which had given to the developing labour movement a remarkable intellectual energy and self-confidence. But is this new science of the 'Machiavellians', as Burnham (1943) called them, superior to Marx's theory of social classes and class conflict?

Marx's theory may be stated briefly in the following propositions:

1 In every society beyond the most primitive, two categories of people may be distinguished:
    (i) a ruling class, and
    (ii) one or more subject classes.
2 The dominant position of the ruling class is to be explained by its possession of the major instruments of economic production, but its political dominance is consolidated by the hold which it establishes over military force and over the production of ideas.
3 There is perpetual conflict between the ruling class and the subject class or classes; and the nature and course of such conflict is influenced primarily by the development of productive forces, i.e. by changes in technology.
4 The lines of class conflict are most sharply drawn in the modern capitalist societies, because in such societies the divergence of economic interests appears most clearly, unobscured by any personal bonds such as those of feudal society, and because the development

of capitalism brings about a more radical polarization of classes than has existed in any other type of society, by its unrivalled concentration of wealth at one extreme of society and of poverty at the other, and by its gradual elimination of the intermediate and transitional social strata.

5 The class struggle within capitalist society will end with the victory of the working class, and this victory will be followed by the construction of a classless socialist society. A number of reasons are advanced for expecting the advent of this form of society:

(i) The tendency of modern capitalism is to create a homogeneous working class, from which it is unlikely that new social divisions will spring in the future.

(ii) The revolutionary struggle of the workers itself engenders cooperation and a sentiment of community, and this sentiment is strengthened by the moral and social doctrines which the revolutionary movement produces, and which have been absorbed into Marx's own thought.

(iii) Capitalism creates the material and cultural preconditions for a classless society – the material conditions by its immense productivity which renders possible the satisfaction of the basic needs of all human beings and removes the edge from the struggle for physical survival, and the cultural conditions by overcoming the 'idiocy of rural life', promoting literacy, diffusing scientific knowledge, and engaging the mass of the people in political life.

Marx's theory was the most comprehensive and systematic which had been propounded in the social sciences up to that time, and in retrospect it is not surprising that for more than a century its influence on social thought and on the development of the labour movement should have been so powerful. Nor is it surprising, on the other hand, that the boldness and range of its generalizations, and the revolutionary doctrine which claimed to be founded upon them, should have attracted so many critical refutations. The lines of criticism have been various. At one level the economic interpretation of history is attacked in very general terms, as a monocausal theory which cannot possibly do justice to the complexity of historical changes. Both Mosca and Pareto argued in this manner, as did Max Weber, but in the course of their argument they extended unjustifiably the scope of Marx's theory. Marx did not say that all social and cultural changes could be explained by economic factors. What he claimed to establish was that the principal types of society, primarily within the area of European civilization, could be distinguished in terms of their economic systems, and that *major* social changes, from one type of society to another, could best be explained by changes in economic activity which brought into existence new social groups with new interests.

A more serious criticism of Marx's theory would consist in showing that one or more of the principal types of society, as defined by him, came into existence, was maintained or declined by the operation of non-economic factors. This is what Schumpeter (1942, pp. 12–13), for example, intended when he drew attention to the difficulty of explaining the rise of European feudalism by economic factors alone, and to the tendency of social institutions to maintain their form in changed economic circumstances:

> Social structures, types and attitudes are coins that do not readily melt. Once they are formed they persist, possibly for centuries, and since different structures and types display different degrees of this ability to survive, we almost always find that actual group and national behaviour more or less departs from what we should expect it to be if we tried to infer it from the dominant forms of the productive process. Though this applies quite generally, it is most clearly seen when a highly durable structure transfers itself bodily from one country to another . . . A related case is of more ominous significance. Consider the emergence of the feudal type of landlordism in the kingdom of the Franks during the sixth and seventh centuries. This was certainly a most important event that shaped the structure of society for many ages and also influenced conditions of production, wants and technology included. But its simplest explanation is to be found in the function of military leadership previously filled by the families and individuals who (retaining that function however) became feudal landlords after the definitive conquest of the new territory.

The emergence of feudal societies, in Europe and elsewhere, does indeed constitute a difficult problem for the Marxist theory, since although these societies can be regarded as resulting immediately from a combination of traditions of military chieftainship with large-scale landownership in a settled agrarian society (and so not entirely excluded from the scope of an economic interpretation of history), nevertheless they appear primarily as political creations, which arise in response to the disintegration of centralized empires.

A still more damaging criticism of Marx's theory, along the same lines, would be one which cast doubt upon the economic interpretation of the origins of modern capitalism, i.e. upon the explanation of the very transition from one type of society to another which Marx examined in the greatest detail and which he thought provided convincing evidence for his theory. The best known of such criticisms is Max Weber's (1904–5) attempt to show that the development of modern capitalism required, besides the economic changes and the formation of a new class which Marx had postulated, a radical change of attitude towards work and the accumulation of wealth, which the Protestant religion brought about. Weber introduced many qualifications into his argument – including the recognition that Protestant doctrines were mainly accepted by those social groups which were already engaged in capitalistic economic activities – but it stands none the less as an attempted refutation of Marx, insofar as it denies that the change from feudalism to capitalism was brought about solely or primarily by economic factors. But how far is Weber's own thesis valid? It has been criticized on various grounds: that it is historically inaccurate in its portrayal of the Protestant ethic, and in its account of the connexions between Protestantism and capitalistic enterprise; and more generally, that it does not provide an independent explanation of the rise of capitalism. In order to do this, Weber would have had to show, not merely that the Protestant ethic was a significant element in the formation of new economic attitudes, but also that no other ideas which were germinating in the circles of the bourgeoisie could have served the same purpose, and that the historical accident of the Reformation was therefore essential to the development of capitalism. In recent years the value of Weber's thesis has come to be more modestly assessed,[1] as emphasizing more strongly than Marx's theory had done (in spite of Marx's analysis of Utilitarianism as the ideology of the bourgeoisie) the importance of ideologies in accelerating or retarding social changes. At the present day, we are perhaps better able to recognize the significance of ideologies in social change, because we have the experience, on the one hand, of the achievements of Marxism itself as an ideology which had an important role in promoting rapid industrialization in the Soviet Union, but also, in its Stalinist version, created a totalitarian society; and on the other hand, of the retarding influence of traditional creeds in some pre-industrial countries.

The value of Marx's concept of the ruling class depends upon the truth of his general social theory. If that theory is not universally valid a ruling class may also be conceived as originating from military power, or in modern times from the power of a political party, as well as from the ownership of the means of production. It may still be maintained, however, that the consolidation of a ruling class requires the concentration of the various types of power – economic, military and political – and that, as a matter of fact, in most societies the formation of this class has begun with the acquisition of economic power. But this raises a more fundamental question about the idea of a ruling class. Is it the case that in every society other than the most simple and primitive this concentration of power occurs, that a ruling class is formed? It should be said at once that the different types of society conform in varying degrees with Marx's model of a society which is clearly divided between a ruling class and subject classes. The most favourable case is probably that of European feudalism, characterized by the rule of a warrior class[2] which had securely in its hands the ownership of land, military force and political authority, and which received the ideological support of a powerful Church. But even here, a number of qualifications are necessary. The idea of a cohesive ruling class is contradicted by the decentralization of political power which was characteristic of feudal societies, and at the stage when this decentralization was overcome – in the absolute monarchies – the European societies were no longer ruled, in a strict sense, by a warrior nobility. Nevertheless, the nobility of the *ancien régime* does come close to the ideal type of a ruling class.

Another case which fits Marx's model well in many respects is that of the bourgeoisie of early capitalism. Its development as an important social class can well be explained by economic changes, and its rise in the economic sphere was accompanied by the acquisition of other positions of power and prestige in society – in politics, administration, the armed forces and the educational system. This conquest of power in the different spheres of society was a long and confused process, which had many local variations in the European countries, and Marx's model was an abstraction from the complex historical reality, bringing together the experiences of the revolution in France – the most violent ideological and political expression of the rise of a new class – and those of the industrial revolution in England. Nevertheless, the pattern of events does conform broadly with Marx's scheme; in England, the Reform Act of 1832 gave political power to the bourgeoisie, and it produced changes in the character of legislation even if it did not, for some considerable time, change the social composition of parliament or cabinets;[3] the reform of the civil service after 1855 opened the way for upper middle-class aspirants to the highest administrative posts;[4] and the development of public schools created new opportunities for children from the newly rich industrial and commercial families to be trained for élite positions. The bourgeoisie also gained powerful ideological support, according to Marx's account, from the political economists and the Utilitarian philosophers.

Nevertheless, the bourgeoisie appears in several respects a less cohesive ruling class than the feudal nobility. It does not actually combine in the same persons military, political and economic power, and there arises the possibility of conflicts of interest between the different groups which represent (as Marx says) the bourgeoisie. Furthermore, capitalist society is more open and mobile than was feudal society; and in the ideological sphere especially, with the development of secular intellectual occupations, conflicting doctrines may arise. Marx expected that the polarization of the two principal classes – the bourgeoisie and industrial working class – would accompany the development of capitalism, and that the rule of the bourgeoisie would become more manifest and more onerous. But this did not happen in the advanced capitalist societies: the different spheres of power have to some extent become more distinct, and the sources of power more numerous and varied; the contrast and opposition between the 'two great classes' of Marx's theory has been modified by the growth of the new middle classes[5] and by a more complex differentiation of occupation and status; and at least since 1945 political rule has generally become milder and less repressive.

One important element in this development has been the gradual attainment, in the twentieth century, of universal adult suffrage, which produces, in principle, a separation between economic and political power. Marx himself considered that the achievement of universal suffrage would be a *revolutionary* step, which would transfer political power to the working class.[6] Thus, whereas the connexion between economic and political power can easily be established in the case of feudal society, or in the case of early capitalism with its limitation of political rights to property owners, it cannot be so easily shown in the case of the modern capitalist democracies, and the notion of a distinct and self-perpetuating ruling class becomes more contentious.

Another important factor has been the development of the postwar welfare state, and increasing intervention by the democratic state in the regulation of economic life, sometimes – especially in Western Europe – in a more 'socialistic' direction through progressive taxation, the extension of public ownership and some degree of economic planning. Nevertheless, in spite of these changes it may be argued that a capitalist class still wields great economic and political power (Bottomore and Brym 1989), and that in some respects this power has increased during the latter part of the twentieth century, economically through the massive concentration of capital in giant corporations, and politically through the growth of the middle classes and the decline in numbers and influence of the traditional working class.

These, in brief, are some of the principal matters of dispute raised by Marx's conception of the ruling class. The value of that conception lies in the rigorous attempt to analyse the sources of political power, and to explain major changes of political regime. With its aid Marx succeeded in expressing in a more exact form an idea which recurs continually in popular thought and in social theory, namely that one of the principal structural features of human societies is their division into a ruling and exploiting group on one side, and subject, exploited groups on the other (Ossowski 1963, chap. 2); in providing an explanation of the causes of this division by connecting in an impressive synthesis a mass of hitherto unrelated economic, political and cultural facts; and in accounting for changes in social structure by the rise and fall of classes. The concept of the 'governing élite' was proposed as an alternative, partly, as we have seen, in order to demonstrate the impossibility of attaining a classless form of society, but also to meet some of the theoretical difficulties which we have just considered. It avoids, in particular, the difficulty of showing that a particular class, defined in terms of its economic position, does in fact dominate all the spheres of social life; but it does so only at the cost of abandoning any attempt to explain the phenomena to which it refers. The governing élite, according to Mosca and Pareto, comprises those who occupy the recognized positions of political power in a society. Thus, when we ask who has power in a particular society, the reply is, those who have power, i.e. those who occupy the specified positions. This is scarcely illuminating; it does not tell us how these particular individuals come to occupy the positions of power. Or else it is misleading; if, for example, those who appear to have power in the formal system of government are in fact subject to the power of other individuals or groups outside this system. Nor does this idea of a governing élite provide much help in the explanation of political changes. Pareto's theory of the circulation of élites, which I shall examine in the next chapter, rests upon assertions about the distribution of psychological characteristics in a population which present numerous difficulties and remain untested in Pareto's own work. Mosca, on the other hand, when he turns to consider the problems of political change, has to introduce the notion of 'social forces' (i.e. important interests in society) as the source of new élites; and as Meisel (1958) commented, this brings him 'uncomfortably close to Marx'.

The difficulties in the concept of a governing élite can be seen most clearly in Mills' (1956) study, which shows the influence of Marx on one side and of Mosca and Pareto on the other. Mills (p. 277) explains his preference for the term 'power élite' rather than 'ruling class' by saying:

'Ruling class' is a badly loaded phrase. 'Class' is an economic term; 'rule' a political one. The phrase 'ruling class' thus contains the theory that an economic class rules politically. That short-cut theory may or may not at times be true, but we do not want to carry that one rather simple theory about in the terms that we use to define our problems; we wish to state the theories explicitly, using terms of more precise and unilateral meaning. Specifically, the phrase 'ruling class', in its common political connotations, does not allow enough autonomy to the political order and its agents, and it says nothing about the military as such ... We hold that such a simple view of 'economic determinism' must be elaborated by 'political determinism' and 'military determinism'; that the higher agents of each of these three domains now often have a noticeable degree of autonomy; and that only in the often intricate ways of coalition do they make up and carry through the most important decisions.

Mills defines the power élite in much the same way as Pareto defined his 'governing élite', saying that 'we may define the power élite in terms of the means of power – as those who occupy the command posts' (p. 23). But the analysis which proceeds from this definition has a number of unsatisfactory features. In the first place, Mills distinguishes three major élites in the USA – the corporation heads, the political leaders and the military chiefs – and he is obliged to go on to enquire whether these three groups together form a single power élite, and if so, what it is that binds them together. One possible answer to these questions is to say that the three groups do form a single élite because they are representatives of an upper class, which has to be regarded, consequently, as a ruling class. But Mills, although he emphasizes that most of the members of these élites are in fact drawn from a socially recognized upper class, says initially that he will leave open the question of whether or not it is such a class which rules through the élites, and when he returns to the problem it is only to reject the Marxist idea of a ruling class in the passage cited above. In short, the question is never seriously discussed, and this is a curious failing in the particular case which Mills is examining, and in the context of the ideas which he is expressing. He had previously rejected the view that there is popular control of the power élite through voting or other means, and emphasized the unity of the élite, as well as the homogeneity of its social origins – all of which points to the consolidation of a ruling class. The formulation which he actually gives is vague and unconvincing: it is a reference to 'the often uneasy coincidence of economic, military, and political power', a coincidence which he proposed to explain largely by the pressures of the international conflict in which the USA was engaged.

Such problems have frequently been raised also in criticisms of Mosca and Pareto. Thus, Friedrich (1950, pp. 259–60) observed that one of the most problematical parts of all élite doctrines is the assumption that the men of power do constitute a cohesive group:

In the light of the continuous change in the composition of the majority, it is not possible to say, under conditions such as prevail in a functioning democracy, that those who play some considerable part in government constitute a cohesive group.

This view of the élite in modern democracies has been widely held and was stated boldly in the conclusions of a study of the upper strata of British society:

> the rulers are not at all close-knit or united. They are not so much in the centre of a solar system, as in a cluster of interlocking circles, each one largely preoccupied with its own professionalism and expertise, and touching others only at one edge ... they are not a single Establishment but a ring of Establishments, with slender connexions. The frictions and balances between the different circles are the supreme safeguard of democracy. No one man can stand in the centre, for there is no centre.[7]

(Sampson 1962, p. 624)

Mills rejected this fashionable liberal-minded doctrine, which he summarized as follows:

> Far from being omnipotent, the élites are thought to be so scattered as to lack any coherence as a historical force ... Those who occupy the formal places of authority are so checkmated – by other élites exerting pressure, or by the public as an electorate, or by constitutional codes – that although there may be upper classes, there is no ruling class; although there may be men of power, there is no power élite; although there may be a system of stratification, it has no effective top.

(1956, pp. 16–17)

As we have seen, he insists that the three principal élites – economic, political and military – are, in fact, a cohesive group, and he supports his view by establishing the similarity of their social origins, the close personal and family relationships between those in the different élites, and the frequency of interchange of personnel between the three spheres. But since he resists the conclusion that the group is a ruling class he is unable to provide a convincing explanation, as distinct from description, of the solidarity of the power élite. Furthermore, by eliminating the idea of a ruling class, he also excludes that of classes in opposition; and so he arrives at an extremely pessimistic account of American society.

The real themes of his book are, first, the transformation of a society in which numerous small and autonomous groups had an effective say in the making of political decisions, into a mass society in which the power élite decides all important issues and keeps the masses quiet by flattery, deception and entertainment; and secondly, the corruption of the power élite itself, which he attributes primarily to a state of affairs in which it is not accountable for its decisions to any organized public, and in which the dominant social value is the acquisition of wealth. Mills' account of the historical changes, which does indeed bring to light some important features of modern politics – the growing political influence of military chiefs, for example – is pessimistic in the sense that it suggests no way out of the situation which it describes and condemns. Like Pareto and Mosca, Mills seems to be saying that if we look at modern societies without illusions we shall see that, however democratic their constitutions, they are in fact ruled by an élite; and to be adding, in a devastating fashion, that even in a society so favourably placed as was the USA at its origins – without a feudal system of ranks, with considerable equality of economic and social condition among its citizens, and with a strongly democratic ideology – the force of events has produced a governing élite of unprecedented power and unaccountability. Where Mills differs from the other Machiavellians is in condemning a state of affairs which they either praised or, in a spirit of disillusionment, accepted.

The concepts of 'ruling class' and 'governing élite' are used in descriptions and explanations of political happenings, and their value must be judged by the extent to which they make possible reasonable answers to important questions about political systems. Do the rulers of society constitute a social group? Is it a cohesive or divided, an open or closed group? How are its members selected? What is the basis of their power? Is this power unrestricted or is it limited by that of other groups in society? Are there significant and regular differences between societies in these respects, and if so, how are they to be explained?

The two concepts are alike in emphasizing the division between rulers and ruled as one of the most important facts of social structure.[8] But they state the division in different ways: the concept of a 'governing élite' contrasts the organized, ruling minority with the unorganized majority, or masses, while the concept of a 'ruling class' contrasts the dominant class with subject classes, which may themselves be organized, or be creating organizations. From these different conceptions arise differences in the way of conceiving the relations between rulers and ruled. In the Marxist theory, which employs the concept of a ruling class, the conflict between classes becomes the principal force producing changes of social structure; but in the élite theories – in spite of the fact that Pareto (1902, vol. II, p. 405) praised highly Marx's conception of class struggle, which he described as 'profoundly true' – the relations between the organized minority and the unorganized majority are necessarily represented as more passive, and the resulting problem of how to explain the rise and fall of ruling élites, if it is confronted at all, has to be dealt with either by postulating a recurrent decadence in the élite (Pareto) or by introducing the idea of the rise of new 'social forces' among the masses (Mosca), which brings the theory close to Marxism.

A further difference between the two concepts lies in the extent to which they make possible explanations of the cohesion of the ruling minority. The 'governing élite', defined as those who occupy the positions of command in a society, is merely assumed to be a cohesive group, unless other considerations, such as their membership of the wealthy class, or their aristocratic family origins are introduced (as they are consistently by Mosca, and occasionally by Pareto). But the 'ruling class', defined as the class which owns the major instruments of economic production in a society, is demonstrated to be a cohesive social group: first, because its members have definite economic interests in common, and, more importantly, because it is engaged permanently in a conflict with other classes in society, through which its self-awareness and solidarity are continually enhanced. Furthermore, this concept states in a precise form what is the basis of the minority's ruling position, namely its economic dominance, while the concept of the 'governing élite' says little about the bases of the power which the élite possesses, except insofar as it incorporates elements from the Marxist theory of classes. In Mills' study of the 'power élite', there is an attempt to explain the power position of the three principal élites taken separately – that of the business executives by the growth in size and complexity of business corporations; that of the military chiefs by the growing scale and expense of the weapons of war, determined by technology and the state of international conflict; and that of the national political leaders, in a somewhat less satisfactory way, by the decline of the legislature, of local politics and of voluntary organizations – but the unity of the power élite as a single group, and the basis of *its* power, are not explained. Why is there *one* power élite and not *three*?

The superiority of the concept of 'ruling class' lies in its greater fertility and suggestiveness and in its value in the construction of theories. But I have pointed out earlier some of the difficulties it encounters, and it is now necessary to consider whether these can be overcome. One important step in this direction might be to give up that view of the concept which treats it as a description of a real phenomenon which is to be observed in all societies in the same general form, and to regard it instead as an 'ideal type', in the sense which Max Weber gave to this term,[9] or as a theoretical model that is open to revision and adaptation. If we treat the concept in this way we can proceed to ask how closely the relationships in a particular society approach the ideal type of a ruling class and subject classes; and so employ the concept, properly, as a tool of thought and investigation. It is then possible to see clearly that the idea of a 'ruling class' originated in the study of a particular historical situation – the end of feudalism and the beginnings of modern capitalism[10] – and to consider how far, and in what respects, other situations diverge from this ideal type, as a result of the absence or weakness of class formation, the influence of factors other than the ownership of property in the creation of classes, and the conflict between different forms of power.

There are two sorts of situation in which we can see especially plainly a divergence from the ideal type of a ruling class. One is that in which, although there is an 'upper class' – that is to say, a clearly demarcated social group which has in its possession a large part of the property of society and receives a disproportionately large share of the national income, and which has created on the basis of these economic advantages a distinctive culture and way of life – this class does not enjoy undisputed or unrestricted political power, in the sense of being able to maintain easily its property rights or to transmit them unimpaired from generation to generation. This kind of situation has been discerned by many observers particularly in the modern democracies, in which, as I noted earlier, there is a potential opposition between the ownership of wealth and productive resources by a small upper class, and the possession of political power, through the franchise, by the mass of the population. As

de Tocqueville once wrote: '*Il est contradictoire que le peuple soit à la fois misérable et souverain.*'

In order to determine whether in such a case there is a 'ruling class' it is necessary first to examine the degree in which the upper class has been successful in perpetuating its ownership of property. We shall have to note, on one side, that in the democratic countries during the present century various restrictions have been placed upon the use of private property, and there has been some reduction in the inequalities of wealth and income, as a result of progressive taxation, and of the growth of publicly owned property and publicly administered social services. On the other side we must note that the decline in the proportion of private wealth owned by the upper class has been fairly modest and very slow, and that the redistribution of income through taxation has not proceeded very far. In England and Wales the top 1 per cent of the population owned 60.9 per cent of national wealth in 1923, and 31.7 per cent in 1972; the top 10 per cent owned 89.1 per cent in 1923, and 70.4 per cent in 1972; while the bottom 80 per cent owned 5.8 per cent in 1923, and 15.1 per cent in 1972 (Pond 1983, p. 11). Later estimates for the United Kingdom indicate that after 1974, and up to the end of the 1970s, the distribution changed very little (ibid., p. 13). The distribution of income in Britain has changed even more modestly, notwithstanding 'progressive taxation': between 1949 and 1978–9 the income share (after tax) of the top 10 per cent declined only from 27.1 per cent to 23.4 per cent, while the share of the bottom 50 per cent changed almost imperceptibly from 26.5 per cent to 26.2 per cent (Playford and Pond 1983, p. 39).[11] Furthermore, during the 1980s there was a sharp reversal of the trend and the available estimates show a marked increase in inequality of wealth and income. The situation in most other capitalist democracies is generally similar (though international comparisons are difficult), but in many of the European countries there has probably not been such a significant growth of inequality during the 1980s as is the case in Britain.

Overall, however, it is evident that the upper class – though with somewhat greater difficulty in countries such as Sweden and Austria – has been able to resist with considerable success the attacks upon its economic interests, and that in this sense of having the power to defend its interests it has maintained itself during the present century as a ruling class. One must be sceptical, therefore, of the view that the extension of voting rights to the mass of the population can establish easily and effectively – or has in fact established in the short period of time in which modern democracies have existed – popular rule, and gradually erode or eliminate the power of a ruling class. What seems to have taken place in the democratic countries up to the present time is not so much a reduction in the power of the upper class as a decline in the radicalism of the working class.

The second type of situation in which there is a divergence from the 'ruling class–subject classes' model is that in which the ruling group is not a class in Marx's sense. One instance is provided by those societies in which a stratum of intellectuals or bureaucrats may be said to wield supreme power – in China under the rule of the *literati*, or in India under the rule of the Brahmins. Another instance is to be found in the former Communist countries where power was concentrated in the leaders of a political party. In these cases, however, we need to examine carefully how far the ruling stratum is clearly distinguishable from a ruling class. In India, the Brahmins, during the ages when they were most powerful, were also substantial landowners, and they were closely allied with the landowning warrior castes in the imperial and feudal periods of India's history. On occasion, they themselves founded ruling or noble houses, and there seems to have been, at times, an amount of movement of individuals and families between the Brahmin and Kshatriya (warrior) castes, which the doctrines of caste exclusiveness expounded in the classical texts do not indicate.

Again, in China, the *literati* were recruited, in the feudal period, from the principal landowning families, and at other times they came in the main from wealthy families (see below, p. 53); so that they were always closely linked with an upper class. There is, moreover, another important economic aspect of the rule of these groups of intellectuals and administrators to which Karl Wittfogel (1957) drew attention. One of the principal instruments of production in China and India (and in a number of other ancient societies; see Steward 1955) was the system of irrigation, and the *literati* and the Brahmins, without owning this property upon which agricultural production depended, still exercised a more or less complete control over its use. Consequently they possessed, in addition to their ownership of land, a vital economic power which, according to Wittfogel, was the principal support of their political dominance.

But notwithstanding these qualifications a distinction remains between social strata of this kind and ruling classes which base their power directly upon the ownership of property. The possession of the means of administration may be, as Max Weber argued, an alternative to the possession of means of economic production, as a basis of political power. This distinction was perhaps more obvious in the case of the Communist countries of Eastern Europe, in which there was little or no private ownership of the principal means of production, and where the leading officials of the ruling party and the state effectively controlled the economy. Wittfogel attempted, in a very ingenious way, to assimilate this type of political power to the general category of 'oriental despotism', but I think the differences are too great – the existence of private ownership of land and other resources, and the intimate bonds between the officials and the property-owning classes in one case, and the specific characteristics of rule by a political party which monopolized power in the other – for this attempt to be successful. The political system as it existed in the Communist countries seems to me to approach the pure type of a 'power élite', that is, of a group which, having come to power with the support or acquiescence of particular classes in the population, maintains itself in power chiefly by virtue of being an organized minority confronting the unorganized majority;[12] whereas in the case of ancient China or India we have to deal with a system which combines the features of a ruling class and a power élite.

There is another element in the position of a ruling class, mentioned previously, which needs to be examined more fully in its bearing upon those situations in which the existence of such a class is doubtful. Since the power of a ruling class arises from its ownership of property, and since this property can easily be transmitted from generation to generation, the class has an enduring character. It is constituted by a group of families which remain as its component elements over long periods of time through the transmission of the family property. Its composition is not entirely immutable, for new families may enter it and old families may decline, but the greater part of its members continue from generation to generation. Only when there are rapid changes in the whole system of production and property ownership does the composition of the ruling class change significantly; and in that case we can say that one ruling class has been replaced by another. If, however, we were to find, in a particular society or type of society, that the movement of individuals and families between the different social levels was so continuous and so extensive that no group of families was able to maintain itself for any length of time in a situation of economic and political pre-eminence, then we should have to say that in such a society there was no ruling class. It is, in fact, this 'circulation of élites' (in the terminology of the élite theorists) or 'social mobility' (in the language of more recent sociological studies) that has been fixed upon by a number of writers as a second important characteristic of modern industrial societies – the first being universal suffrage – which must qualify severely, if it does not altogether exclude, the assertion that there is a ruling class in these societies. By this means we may arrive at the view, which was formulated by Karl Mannheim (1940, part II, chap. 2) among others, that the development of industrial societies can properly be depicted as a movement from a class system to a system of élites, from a social hierarchy based upon the inheritance of property to one based upon merit and achievement. This confrontation between the concepts of 'ruling class' and 'political élite' shows, I think, that while on one level they may be totally opposed, as elements in wide-ranging theories which interpret political life, and especially the future possibilities of political organization, in very different ways, on another level they may be seen as complementary concepts, which refer to different types of political system or to different aspects of the same political system. With their help we can attempt to distinguish between societies in which there is a ruling class, and at the same time élites which represent particular aspects of its interests; societies in which there is no ruling class, but a political élite which founds its power upon the control of the administration, or upon military force, rather than upon property ownership and inheritance; and societies in which there exists a multiplicity of élites among which no cohesive and enduring group of powerful individuals or families seems to be discoverable at all. In order to establish such a classification we need to examine more closely – as I shall do in the following chapters – the circulation of élites, the relations between élites and classes, and the ways in which new élites and new classes are formed.

NOTES

1 See particularly the discussion by Marshall (1982). Weber himself in his later *General Economic History* (1923, part 4) gave a more comprehensive account of the preconditions for the development of capitalism, in which he stressed the rationalization of economic life and referred only briefly to the influence of the Protestant ethic.

2 See the analysis by Marc Bloch (1939–40, vol. II, book III, chap. 1).

3 See Guttsman (1963, chap. 3, 'The changing social structure of the British political élite: 1868–1955').

4 See Kingsley (1944, especially chap. 3, 'Middle class reform: The triumph of plutocracy'). Kingsley concludes that

> the middle classes had by 1870 destroyed the ancien régime on almost every front, [but] the chief gains had been made by the upper ranks of those classes. In the House of Commons wealthy merchants, bankers, industrialists, were displacing the landlords and would begin before many years to replace them in the cabinet. In the Civil Service a somewhat comparable change had occurred. Entrance to the higher posts was no longer a matter of aristocratic influence. The key that now unlocked the door was a costly education which . . . gave to the new system a 'plutocratic character'.
>
> (p. 76)

5 Marx himself, in two passages in *Theories of Surplus Value* (1861–3), recognized the growth of the middle classes, which he described as 'the trend of bourgeois society', but he did not go on to consider the implications of this phenomenon for his general theory. See my discussion of these questions in Bottomore (1991a), and, for a general analysis of the middle classes in advanced capitalist societies, Abercrombie and Urry (1983).

6 Marx (1852):

> We now come to the *Chartists*, the politically active portion of the British *working class*. The six points of the Charter which they contend for contain nothing but the demand of *Universal Suffrage*, and of the conditions without which Universal Suffrage would be illusory for the working class; such as the ballot, payment of members, annual general elections. But Universal Suffrage is the equivalent of political power for the working class of England, where the proletariat forms the large majority of the population, where, in a long, though underground civil war, it has gained a clear consciousness of its position as a class, and where even the rural districts know no longer any peasants, but only landlords, industrial capitalists (farmers) and hired labourers. The carrying of Universal Suffrage in England would, therefore, be a far more socialistic measure than anything which has been honoured with that name on the Continent. Its inevitable result, here, is *the political supremacy of the working class*.

7 A recent thorough study of Britain (Scott 1991) reaches a very different conclusion, which is summarized as follows:

> A ruling class exists when there is both political domination and political rule by a capitalist class. This requires that there be a power bloc dominated by a capitalist class, a power élite recruited from this power bloc, and in which the capitalist class is disproportionately represented, and that there are mechanisms which ensure that the state operates in the interests of the capitalist class and the reproduction of capital. In this sense, I shall show, Britain does still have a ruling class.

> (p. 124)

This kind of analysis and argument is equally applicable to other modern capitalist societies.

8 Mosca (1939, p. 51):

> From the point of view of scientific research the real superiority of the concept of the ruling, or political class lies in the fact that the varying structure of ruling classes has a preponderant importance in determining the political type, and also the level of civilization, of the different peoples.

9 An ideal type concept

> brings together certain relationships and events of historical life into a complex which is conceived as an internally consistent system ... this construction itself is like a utopia which has been arrived at by the analytical accentuation of certain elements of reality ... it *is* no hypothesis but it offers guidance in the construction of hypotheses. It is not a *description* of reality but it aims to give unambiguous means of expression to such a description ... An ideal type is formed by the one-sided *accentuation* of one or more points of view and by the synthesis of a great many diffuse, discrete, more or less present and occasionally absent *concrete individual* phenomena, which are arranged according to those one-sidedly emphasized viewpoints into a unified *analytical* construct.

> (Weber 1904, p. 90)

10 As Croce (1913, p. 17) argued concerning the whole theory of historical materialism: 'The materialistic view of history arose out of the need to account for a definite social phenomenon, not from an abstract inquiry into the factors of historical life.'

11 See also the earlier study by Titmuss (1962), which concluded that

> we should be much more hesitant in suggesting that any equalizing forces at work in Britain since 1938 can be promoted to the status of a 'natural law' and projected into the future. As we have shown, there are often forces, deeply rooted in the social structure and fed by many complex institutional factors inherent in large-scale economies, operating in reverse

directions. Some of the more critical of these factors, closely linked with the distribution of power, and containing within themselves the seeds of long-lasting effects – as, for instance, in the case of settlements and trusts – function as concealed multipliers of inequality. They are not measured at present by the statistics of income and only marginally by the statistics of wealth. Even so, there is more than a hint from a number of studies that income inequality has been increasing since 1949 whilst the ownership of wealth, which is far more highly concentrated in the United Kingdom than in the United States, has probably become still more unequal and, in terms of family ownership, possibly strikingly more unequal, in recent years.

(p. 198)

12 For a more extensive analysis, see Bottomore (1991a, chap. 3).

Chapter 3

Politics and the circulation of élites

'History is a graveyard of aristocracies' (Pareto 1915–19, p. 1430). In this graphic phrase, Pareto formulated one of the fundamental ideas of his political theory – the 'circulation of élites'. But in his major works the analysis of the phenomenon is less impressive than the glamour of the style. There are two principal difficulties to be confronted. In the first place, does the 'circulation of élites' refer to a process in which *individuals* circulate between the élite and the non-élite, or to a process in which *one élite* is replaced by another? Both conceptions are to be found in Pareto's work, although the former predominates. When, for example, he discusses the decay and renewal of aristocracies, he observes that 'the governing class is restored not only in numbers but – and that is the more important thing – in quality, by families rising from the lower classes' (ibid.)[1] Pareto refers again and again to this phenomenon, using similar expressions – 'the circulation of individuals between the two strata (élite and non-élite)' (ibid., p. 1427); 'in the higher stratum of society, Class II residues gradually lose in strength, until now and again they are reinforced by tides upwelling from the lower stratum' (ibid.). At the same time, Pareto refers to another kind of social movement which is of vital importance for the equilibrium of society, and which consists in the emergence and rise to power of new élites. He appears to connect this movement with a failure of circulation in the first sense, but it is evident that he also regards it as an aspect of the circulation of élites in general. In *Les systèmes socialistes* he observes that

    a slowing down of this circulation [of individuals] may result in a considerable increase of the degenerate elements in the classes which still hold power, and on the other hand, in an increase of elements of superior quality in the subject classes. In such a case, the social equilibrium becomes unstable . . . and the slightest shock will destroy it. A conquest or a revolution produces an upheaval, brings a new élite to power, and establishes a new equilibrium.

(vol. 1, p. 30)

The various types of circulation of élites were differentiated more precisely by one of Pareto's pupils, Marie Kolabinska, in a work entitled *La circulation des élites en France* (1912) which was cited with approbation by the master himself. Kolabinska distinguishes three types of circulation. First, there is the circulation which takes place between different categories of the governing élite itself. Secondly, there is the circulation between the élite and the rest of the population, which may take either of two forms: (i) individuals from the lower strata may succeed in entering the existing élite, or (ii) individuals in the lower strata may form new élite groups which then engage in a struggle for power with the existing élite. The major part of Kolabinska's work is devoted to a study of these last two processes in French society in the period between the eleventh and the eighteenth centuries, and I shall consider its findings later.

The second difficulty in Pareto's exposition concerns his explanation of the circulation of élites. On some occasions he seems to regard élites as representing particular social interests, and the circulation of élites as resulting from the decline of established interests and the rise of new interests. Thus, he observes that 'in the beginning, military, religious, and commercial aristocracies and plutocracies – with a few exceptions not worth considering – must have constituted parts of the governing élite and sometimes have made up the whole of it' (1915–19, p. 1430). Elsewhere, in discussing the rise of new élites, he notes that the industrial workers in England have produced a trade union élite (1902, vol. 1, pp. 32–3). This type of explanation is set out more explicitly by Kolabinska, who cites as examples of rising élite groups in different periods of French history the commercial classes, the industrial classes, the bourgeoisie, lawyers and financiers.

It is clear, however, that Pareto intends to explain the circulation of élites mainly by changes in the psychological characteristics of members of the élite on one side, and of the lower strata on the other; or, as he puts it, by the changes in the residues occurring within the two strata. Aristocracies, he says, do not decline only in numbers:

> They decay also in quality, in the sense that they lose their vigour, that there is a decline in the proportions of the residues which enabled them to win their power and hold it. The governing class is restored . . . by families rising from the lower classes.
>
> (1915–19, p. 1430)

Again, in discussing the circulation of whole groups, Pareto suggests that revolutions come about through the accumulation of decadent elements in the higher strata of society, and the increase of elements of superior quality in the lower strata (ibid., p. 1431). In order to assess the value of this explanation it is necessary to consider briefly Pareto's concept of 'residues'. He begins (ibid., chap. 2) by making a distinction between the logical and non-logical actions ('rational' and 'non-rational' would be more suitable terms) of individuals in social life: logical actions are those directed to attainable ends and employing means which are appropriate to the attainment of the ends; non-logical actions are those not directed to any end, or directed to unattainable ends, or using means which cannot attain the end. Pareto takes the view that most human actions are non-logical,[2] and he goes on to enquire what the forces are behind non-logical action and how it comes to be represented, as frequently happens, as logical action. These forces he discovers in six 'residues', which he calls residues of combinations (I), of the persistence of aggregates (II), of sociability (III), of activity (IV), of the integrity of the individual (V) and of sex (VI) (ibid., chaps 6–8). The ways in which the actions determined by these residues assume the appearance of logical actions are discussed by Pareto under the heading of 'derivations' (ibid., chaps 9–10), which bear some resemblance to 'ideologies' in Marx's sense. Pareto does not define the residues very precisely, and he uses them capriciously in his descriptions of social events.[3] In the final part of the book (chaps 12–13), where he treats more comprehensively the problem of the circulation of élites and social equilibrium, he makes use of only the first two classes of residues. The rule of the governing élite, he argues, may be of two kinds: it may be maintained either by cunning (predominance of residues of combination) or by force (predominance of residues of the persistence of aggregates). Residues I and II are thus treated as categories within which all political attitudes can be classified, and the greater part of Pareto's discussion of political life amounts to an attempt to fit selected data of the history of Western societies into this scheme. It is a remarkably simple classification, especially when considered in relation to the huge edifice of concepts which Pareto constructed in the earlier parts of his treatise; and it hardly shows any striking originality. Pareto's two types of élite, animated by residues I and II respectively – types which he also refers to as the 'speculators' and the 'rentiers' – bear a close resemblance to Machiavelli's 'foxes' and 'lions', but they are dressed up in a more scientific garb. Whether they are actually more scientific terms is open to doubt, for while there is a great parade of scientific method throughout Pareto's treatise, little or no attempt is made to establish by exact methods of investigation that the two kinds of personality which are alleged to determine the character-istics of these types of élite actually exist, to describe them precisely in psychological terms, or to show that there are no other varieties of political personality. Even if the existence of such personality types, and their significance in political life, were assumed, it would still be necessary to show that the changes in states of mind and feeling, in ideas and sentiments, among the members of the élite occur independently of social changes, and in turn produce the circulation of élites. This Pareto does not attempt to do; instead, he takes historical examples of declining élites and then simply asserts that there has been a change in their 'residues'.

Pareto's study of the rise and decline of élites as such is equally unsatisfactory. He does not attempt to assemble all the available instances (even for limited periods) and to show that there are regularities in élite circulation which might be connected with changes in sentiments, supposing that the latter could be independently established. He produces only historical illustrations, drawn mainly from contemporary Italian politics and from the history of ancient Rome, to support his general arguments.

Lastly, Pareto does not resolve the question of how the two types of élite circulation – the ascent and descent of individuals, and the rise and fall of social groups – are connected with each other. He suggests, briefly, that if the governing élite is relatively open to superior individuals from the lower strata it has a better chance of enduring,[4] and conversely, that the replacement of one élite by another may result from a failure in this circulation of individuals. Thus, he claims that:

> Revolutions come about through accumulations in the higher strata of society – either because of a slowing down in class circulation, or from other causes – of decadent elements no longer possessing the residues suitable for keeping them in power, or shrinking from the use of force; while meantime in the lower strata of society elements of superior quality are coming to the fore, possessing residues suitable for exercising the functions of government and willing enough to use force.

> (1915–19, p. 1431)

The reader will look in vain, however, for substantial evidence in support of these propositions, either from a comparative study of revolutions, or from a systematic comparison between societies which show important differences in the degree of circulation of individuals between the élite and the non-élite.

It is true that the data for such comparisons would be difficult to assemble, but there are historical examples which appear at once to invalidate Pareto's generalization. One such instance is that of India – a society which had, over long periods, an extremely rigid form of stratification and, so far as can be discovered, relatively little movement of individuals from the lower strata of society into the élite; but which yet experienced until modern times few revolutionary movements, and none which resulted in the replacement of one élite by another. Even if we concede that in modern Western societies it may be useful to look for a connexion between the amount of social mobility and the prevalence of revolutionary sentiments and activities, it is still not possible to explain the rise and fall of élites, whether this occurs through revolutionary or through more gradual changes, solely by the restrictions upon the movement of individuals into the élite. It is necessary to examine some of those 'other causes' which Pareto mentions but does not investigate.

The work of Marie Kolabinska (1912) on élites in France was intended to demonstrate the truth of Pareto's theory by a closer study of the process of circulation in a single society. In fact, however, it provides no empirical evidence more convincing than that which Pareto's own excursions into history supply, for it employs the same inadequate method of historical illustration. For each of the periods of French history which she surveys Kolabinska cites examples of the rise or fall of particular individuals or families, but although this reveals that *some* individuals were able to change their social rank in French society during these times (and who doubted it?) it tells us nothing about the extent of such circulation, and it cannot therefore enable us to relate the volume of circulation to significant changes in the economic or political system. Only in dealing with the final period (1715–89) covered by her study does she provide any quantitative indications concerning the representation of different social strata in the élites; and even then the material which she assembles is very slight and is interpreted in a way which arouses doubts as to its significance. Thus, she quotes at one point (p. 93) a remark that in 1787 one-fifth of the higher cavalry officers did not belong to the titled nobility, and that some of them did not even have the nobiliary particle '*de*' in their names, as evidence that commoners were gaining access to the military élite; yet in the very next chapter she suggests that the French élites, including the military élite, were becoming more exclusive in the years immediately preceding the Revolution, and she cites another author to the effect that the absence of the nobiliary particle was no proof at all that an individual was of non-noble birth (p. 104). It may be noted, further, that Kolabinska, who made her investigation before the publication of Pareto's *Treatise*, was happily dispensed from the obligation to explore the connexion between the fortunes of those individuals whose careers she traces, and their 'residues', and her explanation of these movements is therefore given largely in terms of the development of new economic interests.

The same phenomena of élite circulation have been studied by a number of other writers to whose work we can turn for alternative accounts of how and why it occurs. Mosca (1884, pp. 30–1) described it in the following terms in his earliest book:

> When the aptitude to command and to exercise political control is no longer the sole possession of the legal rulers but has become common enough among other people; when outside the ruling class another class has formed which finds itself deprived of power though it does

have the capacity to share in the responsibilities of government – then that law has become an obstacle in the path of an elemental force and must, by one way or another, go.

The same idea is formulated again in his later work (1896, p. 116):

within the lower classes another ruling class, or directing minority, necessarily forms, and often this new class is antagonistic to the class that holds possession of the legal government.

Mosca also recognizes, besides this form of circulation which consists in the struggle between élites and the replacement of an old élite by a new one, that other form which consists in the renewal of the existing élite by the accession of individuals from the lower classes of society; and he examines in a number of different contexts the relative ease or difficulty of access to the élite. He is led from this to distinguish between mobile and immobile societies, according to the degree of openness of the élite, and in contrast with Pareto he notices, and indeed exaggerates, as a significant characteristic of modern democratic societies the considerable volume of movement between the different social levels. In the modern European societies

the ranks of the ruling classes have been held open. The barriers that kept individuals of the lower classes from entering the higher have been either removed or lowered, and the development of the old absolutist state into the modern representative state has made it possible for almost all political forces, almost all social values, to participate in the management of society.

(1939, p. 474)

The most prominent feature in Mosca's treatment of the circulation of élites is to be seen, however, in the kind of explanation which he seeks. He refers occasionally to the intellectual and moral qualities of the members of the élite, but unlike Pareto he does not attach supreme importance to these psychological characteristics. In the first place, he observes that such individual characteristics are frequently produced by social circumstances:

Courage in battle, impetuousness in attack, endurance in resistance – such are the qualities that have long and often been vaunted as a monopoly of the higher classes. Certainly there may be vast natural and – if we may say so – innate differences between one individual and another in these respects; but more than anything else traditions and environmental influences are the things that keep them high, low or just average, in any large group of human beings.

(ibid., p. 64)

Secondly, he makes scarcely any reference to such individual characteristics in his explanation of the rise and fall of élites; he explains these phenomena by the germination of new interests and ideals in a society, as well as by the appearance of new problems:

What we see is that as soon as there is a shift in the balance of political forces – when, that is, a need is felt that capacities different from the old should assert themselves in the management of the state, when the old capacities, therefore, lose some of their importance or changes in their distribution occur – then the manner in which the ruling class is constituted changes also. If a new source of wealth develops in a society, if the practical importance of knowledge grows, if an old religion declines or a new one is born, if a new current of ideas spreads, then, simultaneously, far-reaching dislocations occur in the ruling classes.

(ibid., p. 65)

As Meisel noted (above, p. 22), this line of argument brings Mosca close to Marxist ideas, and since he is aware of the danger he tries strenuously to distinguish his theory from that of Marx by insisting upon the limitations of the economic interpretation of history and emphasizing the influence of moral and religious ideas in social change. Mosca's position on this question is, in fact, not very different from that of Max Weber, in rejecting an exclusive and one-sided economic interpretation of history; but he is less willing than Weber was to recognize the importance of Marx's thought.

Two other writers discussed, quite independently, the problem of the circulation of élites, and we may briefly consider their views at this stage. The Belgian historian, Henri Pirenne (1914), in an essay on the social history of capitalism,[5] advanced the hypothesis that each distinct period in the development of capitalism[6] was characterized by the dominance of a different group of capitalists:

With every change in economic development, there is a break in continuity. The capitalists who have been active up to that point recognize, one may say, that they are incapable of adapting themselves to the circumstances produced by hitherto unknown needs, which require new means for their satisfaction. They retire from the struggle, and become an aristocracy whose members, if they participate at all in the management of affairs, participate only in a passive way by providing capital. In their place new men arise, bold and enterprising individuals who sail audaciously before the winds of change.

(1914)

Pirenne distinguishes four main periods in which such transformations occurred – the rise of the town merchants from the eleventh century, the development of international trade in the thirteenth century, the emergence of new industries and of manufacturing towns in the sixteenth century, and finally the industrial revolution of the eighteenth century – and attempts to show that at each of these turning points new men rose from the lower strata of society to become the leaders of economic activity.

Some similar observations are made by Schumpeter (1927) in his essay on social classes, where he distinguishes very clearly between different types of circulation in those sections which deal with 'the rise and fall of families within a class', 'movement across class lines' and 'the rise and fall of whole classes'. One valuable feature of Schumpeter's study is that it considers together both the individual and the social factors in the circulation of élites. In the movement of families between classes, he argues, social ascent is influenced – leaving aside the operation of chance – by individual endowment in energy and intelligence, but also by social circumstances such as the openness of the upper class, and the opportunities for enterprise in new fields of activity. Similarly, in the rise and fall of whole classes, some weight must be attributed to the qualities of individuals, but a more important influence is exerted by structural changes affecting the functions of the different groups:

the position of each class in the total national structure depends on the one hand, on the significance that is attributed to [its] function, and, on the other hand, on the degree to which the class successfully performs the function.

(ibid., p. 180)

Schumpeter illustrates this process by an examination of the rise of a warrior nobility in Germany, and its subsequent decline from the end of the fourteenth century as a result of the development of a national administrative system, and of the patrimonialization of landed property. The underlying causes of this decline are to be found in the loss in social importance of the function of individual combat – the demilitarization of society – and in the economic changes which favoured large landed estates.[7]

The foregoing studies were all intended to contribute in some way to the understanding of political change, either by accounting for changes in the personnel of the formal institutions of government, or in a broader sense, by explaining the fluctuations in the power or influence of particular groups in society. How far were they successful in formulating the main problems and in producing evidence to support their conclusions? There are far-reaching differences between Pareto's approach and that which was adopted by Mosca, Pirenne or Schumpeter. Pareto devotes most attention to the circulation of individuals between the élite and the non-élite; and this preoccupation follows directly from his choice of 'social equilibrium' as the main subject of his investigation. Like the modern functionalists – one of whose principal ancestors he is in an ideological as well as a scientific sense – Pareto sets out to study those factors which maintain a particular society, or a particular form of society, in existence; and, like them again, he tacitly excludes from his field of research any enquiry into the major differences between types of society or into the causes of change from one type of society to another. In Pareto's historical picture there are no real transformations of social structure but only an endless cyclical movement in which a declining élite is restored to vitality by the recruitment of new elements from the lower strata of the population, or is overthrown and replaced by a new élite which has been formed by these same elements in conditions where they are denied access, as individuals, to the established élite. Through all these movements the form of society remains unchanged, since it is defined abstractly as the rule of an élite over the majority of the population. There can be no sense in asking, from the standpoint which Pareto takes, whether there have been historical changes in the composition and cultural outlook of the élite, or in the relations between the élite and the masses. Whenever Pareto touches upon problems such as these, he at once recoils, and reaffirms that the main theme of his study is the general, abstract and *a*historical question of the conditions of social equilibrium.

Mosca, Pirenne and Schumpeter, on the contrary, although they differ on many points, agree in recognizing that new social groups may be formed in a society as a result of economic or cultural changes, that such groups may then increase their social influence insofar as the kinds of activity in which they engage become of vital importance to society at large, and that these activities may in due course produce changes in the political system, and in the social structure as a whole. Their concern with the rise and fall of social groups, and particularly of those groups which are distinguished by their economic functions, shows the influence of Marx's theory of classes; and the same influence is apparent in the fact that they apply the term 'class' rather than 'élite' to such groups, and so present a model of society in which the complexity and historical variability of class structure figures more prominently than does the universal and unchanging division between a ruling élite and the masses. It is only in Mosca's work that the latter distinction finds a place at all, and as I showed earlier it is largely abandoned when he comes to discuss the political systems of modern societies. This is not to say that any of these writers wholly neglects the circulation of individuals between the élite groups (or upper class) and the lower strata of society, in his concern with the movement of social groups. Schumpeter, as we have seen, makes a very careful distinction between these different types of circulation, and so, in a less clear-cut fashion, does Mosca; only Pirenne, in this particular study, confines his attention to the formation of new classes. But on this point, too, they differ markedly from Pareto, since (as Schumpeter's work makes especially clear) they explain the circulation of individuals and families within the class system very largely by characteristics of the class structure itself, rather than by individual differences of ability and character. The most distinctive feature of this conception of the circulation of élites – and this follows from the points I have already mentioned – is that it takes account of a real historical development, at least within the area of Western civilization, in the nature of élites, and of their relations with the rest of society, and accepts that the changes in technology, and in general culture, have produced different forms of class structure and of political power.

But although we can find, in the works of Mosca, Pirenne and Schumpeter, a more coherent account and more plausible explanations of the circulation of élites than is to be discovered in the writings of Pareto, these studies are still inadequate in many respects. One of their most obvious deficiencies is the lack of a proper method of investigation. Not one of these studies makes it possible to establish that there is, or is not, a constant connexion between the amount of circulation of individuals and groups in society and the extent of changes in the economic, political and cultural system: first, because they present no systematic comparisons between societies, and secondly, because they provide no exact measurement of the phenomena with which they deal. Pareto, Mosca, Kolabinska, Pirenne and Schumpeter all succeed in showing (as is not very difficult to do) that some individuals change their class position, or move between the élite and the non-élite. They do this, in the main, by giving examples of individuals who have risen in the social hierarchy. But this does not tell us what we need most to know: namely, what *proportion* of the élite or upper class is recruited from the lower strata of society, and what proportion of those in the lower strata is enabled to rise.

The outcome of this method of historical illustration seems very often to be an inflation of the amount of circulation in a society. William Miller (1962), for example, has noted that historians, dealing with one aspect of élite recruitment during a recent period of American history, have greatly exaggerated the proportion of business leaders who rose from the lower strata of society:

> Virtually all the generalizations that go to make up this model [of recruitment to the business élite] are based upon a few remarkable life histories from the 'robber baron' period ... Yet to read the lives of business leaders ... is to look almost in vain for working class or foreign origins, and even poor and unschooled farm boys are not conspicuous among such leaders.[8]

(pp. 319, 321)

It is clear that exact measurement of the circulation of individuals between the élite and the non-élite (which forms part of the study of what modern sociologists call 'social mobility') presents great difficulties, even when it is undertaken in present-day societies. Some of these difficulties were indicated in S. M. Miller's (1960) attempt to study social mobility on a comparative basis, and in the later study by Heath (1981): leaving aside a host of general problems of measurement, there are particular difficulties which arise from variations in the size of élites between one society and another, and from differences in the class structure of societies, which may have quite different proportions of their population in agricultural or industrial work, and in manual or non-manual occupations.

One conclusion which emerges from considering these problems is that a simple distinction between the élite and the non-élite, such as Pareto used, is quite inadequate, for no calculation of the rate of movement into the élite from other sections of the population is likely to be meaningful unless we know something about the size and structure of the élite, and about the general class structure, in a particular society. However, in the study of the circulation of élites in present-day societies it is at least possible to collect much of the necessary data, through national sample surveys or through more intensive studies of particular élite groups. When we turn to historical studies of élite circulation the collection of data itself constitutes a further difficulty, which was not seriously confronted by the earlier writers. The present lack of information is no doubt due, in part, to the fact that general historians have not usually been interested in this kind of quantitative investigation, and that social history, which would concern itself with these problems, is a fairly recent discipline. As William Miller observes in the essay quoted earlier:

> One might have supposed that historians, largely occupied as they have been with the activities of ruling classes, would have been among the first to study systematically the problems of the recruitment and tenure of élites. This problem is an especially interesting one in a country such as the United States which has had no official caste systems and no legally established hereditary hierarchies. Yet most American historians have shied away from it.
>
> (1962, p. 309)

The studies of the business élite in the volume which Miller edited (1962), a study of the Chinese *literati* (Marsh 1961), some other historical studies (Dent 1973, Jaher 1973), and studies of the political élite in various countries (Guttsman 1963, Marvick 1961) indicate that the necessary historical information can in some cases be discovered; but it may well be that, for many countries and periods, it will remain impossible to determine in any exact way how much movement there has been into and out of the élite.

Even if reasonably exact information about the circulation of élites in a large number of societies were made available, it would still be necessary, in order to demonstrate a connexion between this circulation and other social phenomena, to take a step which none of the earlier writers on élites attempted: namely, to undertake comprehensive and systematic comparisons between societies. Pareto suggests that the circulation of individuals between the élite and the non-élite is a constant and regular phenomenon. But is this so? Are there not substantial differences between societies in the rate of circulation? And if this is so, what are the causes of these differences and what are their effects in the political sphere? Mosca and others suggest that the rate of circulation is particularly high in modern societies, and that, in Mosca's words, 'the modern representative state has made it possible for almost all political forces, almost all social values, to participate in the management of society' (1939, p. 474). The investigations which I have just discussed do not entirely confirm this view, but the modern industrial societies may still be a good deal more mobile than most other types of society. Another question which we may put concerns the relation between individual mobility and the rise and fall of élites or classes. Is it true, as Pareto argues, that revolutions occur when the rate of circulation of individuals is too low? These questions indicate an array of problems which can certainly not be solved on the basis of present knowledge, and which the early writers only posed, although they expressed themselves in what purported to be explanatory statements.

Pareto, as we have seen, focused his attention upon this movement of individuals in the circulation of élites. The other writers, who dealt at greater length with the movement of groups – the rise and fall of élites – do not seem to me to have advanced very far beyond what Marx had already accomplished in accounting for the origins and development of social classes. In fact, they all attribute prime importance to the emergence of new interests in society. Mosca's 'social forces' are very like Marx's 'class interests', Pirenne deals entirely with the rise of new groups of capitalists, and Schumpeter explains the decline of an armed nobility very largely in economic terms. Where they diverge from

Marxism is in dealing much more thoroughly with the development of sub-groups within the major social classes – new occupational groups, for instance – and, of course, in refraining from any discussion of the potential classless society which Marx discerned within modern capitalism. Mosca, although he insists so strongly upon the influence of cultural and religious factors in the creation of new 'social forces', does not produce or examine closely any historical instances which might bear out his claim that factors of this kind are sometimes of crucial importance in bringing about changes in the social structure. Schumpeter, in his later work (1942), discusses the changes in culture which are helping to bring about the decline of capitalism, but for the most part treats these changes as secondary in relation to the changes in the economic order.

There is one question, in particular, which these writers fail to examine with even such close attention as Marx himself: namely, the nature and causes of revolutionary changes in society. This problem needs to be set out in broader terms than those which Marx – in his preoccupation with the nineteenth-century revolutions – employed. In the rise and fall of social groups two processes may be observed: one in which there is a gradual acquisition of the positions of power by individuals belonging to a new social stratum, sometimes through alliances with members of the established political élite; and another in which there is a violent confrontation between a rising social group and the established rulers of society. One of the objects of political studies is to discover, so far as possible, the conditions and causes of these different types of circulation of social groups. Pareto hardly touches upon the problem, and his observations upon revolutions are sparse and disconnected. Mosca, on the other hand, devotes a chapter of *The Ruling Class* (1939, chap. 8) to the subject of revolution, but it is one of the most disappointing sections of his work, providing little more than a descriptive account of a few revolutionary periods.

It cannot be said that the work of other sociologists, after Marx, has added much to the explanation of revolutionary changes, in spite of the abundance of material supplied by our own revolutionary century. One comprehensive and systematic discussion of these questions is that by Brinton (1957), who distinguishes as conditions which favour revolutionary change: economic progress in a society, bitter class antagonisms, desertion of the ruling class by the intellectuals, inefficient governmental machinery and a politically inept ruling class. The conditions do not differ widely from those which Marx proposed at various times, especially in his early writings, except that the formation of the revolutionary class itself receives much less attention; but they are set out as a framework for a more rigorous comparative study. The usefulness of this conceptual framework may be seen by applying it to the revolutions of the twentieth century, most of which have occurred in industrially backward countries, which possessed in a high degree the characteristics that Brinton distinguishes: extreme class antagonisms produced by the immense differences between the rich and the poor, the defection of Westernized intellectuals, frequently influenced by Marxism, and the ineptitude of traditional ruling groups in dealing with economic problems and with the impact of more advanced societies.

One conclusion that emerges clearly from most of these later studies of the subject, and which confirms Marx's theory, is that modern revolutions cannot be explained by the activities of small élite groups. They have been brought about by the actions of a whole class or an alliance of classes, whose role has to be seen, however, in a broader framework involving the international context – especially the association between war and revolution – and the potential autonomy of state structures which is emphasized by Skocpol (1979). Classes, of course, have leaders, but any élite group of leaders arises from, and to some extent along with, the formation and development of the class – it does not create the class, nor does it by itself bring about a revolutionary movement. The same is true, I think, in the case of more gradual changes in the position of groups in the hierarchy of power. It is because the situation of relatively large groups in the population changes that new élites can be formed and can, over a period of time, wrest a share in political power from the established rulers of society.

In studying the circulation of groups, as in studying the circulation of individuals, we have to confront many difficulties in the collection of data. The two studies overlap to some extent, and present the same problems, for it may be necessary to trace the movement of individuals in order to throw light upon the formation of new social groups or the decline of old ones. In most cases, however, it is somewhat easier to discover evidence for the rise and fall of social groups, because their existence and activities are likely to be documented in legal texts or in contemporary chronicles, or they may be inferred from a knowledge of other social institutions, such as systems of land tenure, property ownership, and religious or military organization. But whichever aspect of the circulation of élites attracts our attention we can supplement historical knowledge of the phenomenon (and such knowledge could itself be greatly extended) by studies of the social movements of the twentieth century – studies which were beyond the powers of the earlier writers on élites. During the last forty years the circulation of élites in the industrial societies has been the object of numerous investigations, and the same attention has been given to it more recently in the so-called developing countries. A review of the accumulated evidence from several societies of each type, which I shall undertake in the following two chapters, may enable us to formulate some more adequately supported generalizations than those which have been criticized here.

NOTES

1 The idea is stated in almost identical terms in his earlier book (1902, vol. 2, pp. 28–30).
2 According to Pareto the principal spheres of logical action are the economic (or business) and the scientific. He exaggerates the rationality of behaviour in these spheres, especially in the first, and underrates the degree of rationality in other forms of social action, e.g. in politics.
3 The concept of 'residues' was criticized at length by Ginsberg (1936) in an essay on 'The sociology of Pareto' which makes very plain the vagueness and inadequacy of Pareto's ideas on this subject.
4 Cf. Kolabinska (1912, p. 9): 'In general, the élites which receive elements from outside themselves are in a better position to endure than those which exclude such elements.'
5 *Bulletin de l'Académie royale de Belgique*, mai 1914. An English version, which omitted many of the footnotes, was published in the *American Historical Review*, April 1914.
6 It does not affect the present discussion that Pirenne discovers the origins of this development in a very early period, namely the eleventh century.
7 For a critical discussion of Schumpeter's class theory as a whole, see Bottomore (1992, chap. 4).
8 This view is confirmed by a comparative study of the recruitment of élites by S. M. Miller (1960), which concludes that no country among the fourteen for which data were available had any considerable movement from the manual strata of the population into the upper levels.

Chapter 4

Intellectuals, managers and bureaucrats

Among the social groups which have risen to prominence in the tremendous social and political changes of the twentieth century, three élites – the intellectuals, the managers of industry and the high government officials – have often been singled out as the inheritors of the functions of earlier ruling classes and as vital agents in the creation of new forms of society. But how important have they really been in initiating change? How far are they the products of other, more fundamental, changes in society, and representatives of more powerful interests? Let us be clear at the outset that the attribution of such great social influence to these élite groups derives in the first place from the acceptance of the general theory of élites, and springs directly from the critique of Marxism which that theory supplied. For according to the Marxist view the most significant fact of Western history since the mid-nineteenth century is the rise of the working class as a new social force; while the accounts which are given of the rise of the intellectuals, or managers, or bureaucrats, all challenge that view, and attempt to show that the transformations of capitalism lead to a 'classless' recruitment of élites (i.e. a more or less perfect circulation of individuals between the various levels of prestige and power), but at the same time maintain in existence the distinction between a ruling élite and the masses (i.e. do not lead towards a classless society). In examining the rise of these élites, therefore, we shall need to consider, first, how they are related to the major social classes, and what modifications they have brought about in the class system of the capitalist countries, and secondly, what was the nature of their role in collectivist societies as they existed in Eastern Europe.

Of these three groups the intellectuals are the most difficult to define, and their social influence is the most difficult to determine. We may begin by distinguishing between 'intellectuals' and 'intelligentsia'. The latter term was first used in Russia in the nineteenth century to refer to those who had received a university education which qualified them for professional occupations; subsequently, its denotation has been extended by many writers, to include almost all those who are engaged in non-manual occupations. In this sense it is equivalent to the 'new middle classes', within which we may distinguish between higher and lower strata – the higher comprising those in professional, technical and higher managerial occupations, and the lower those in the more routine clerical and administrative jobs. The intellectuals, on the other hand, are generally regarded as comprising the much smaller group of those who contribute directly to the creation, transmission and criticism of cultural products and ideas; they include writers, artists, scientists and technologists, philosophers, religious thinkers, social theorists, political commentators. The boundaries of the group may be difficult to determine with precision, and its lower levels merge with middle-class occupations such as teaching and journalism, but its characteristic feature – direct concern with the culture of a society – is sufficiently clear.

Intellectuals of one sort or another are to be found in almost all societies – in non-literate societies as magicians and priests, poets and minstrels, or genealogists, and in literate societies as philosophers, writers, teachers, scientists, high officials, lawyers, and so on – but their functions and their social importance vary considerably. In some societies the intellectuals have come close to being a governing élite. In China the *literati* formed, over long periods, a ruling stratum of this kind, which according to Max Weber (1920) grew out of an education for genteel laymen. It was not a hereditary or exclusive group, since entry to it was by public competitive examination; but in practice it was largely recruited, during the feudal period, from important feudal families, and later on, from the higher social strata (including a high proportion of officials' families). Nevertheless, a statistical analysis (Marsh 1961) of the *literati* in the period 1600–1900 indicates that some 30 per cent were recruited from the families of commoners; i.e. from a social level below the élite, although some of them certainly came from wealthy families. In India, a similar situation existed in the sense that the Brahmins constituted themselves a ruling stratum in the society; but there are important differences from the case of China, for the Brahmins were a hereditary caste, and their training was religious rather than literary. On the other hand, the clerics occupied a less dominant position in the European feudal societies, and only with the breakdown of feudalism did the intellectuals begin to assume a more important social role.

The origins of the modern intellectuals have generally been placed in the universities of medieval Europe (Le Goff 1957, Mannheim 1956). The growth of the universities, associated with the spread of humanistic learning, made possible the formation of an intellectual stratum which was not a priestly caste, whose members were recruited from diverse social milieux, and which was in some measure detached from the ruling classes and ruling doctrines of feudal society. This intellectual stratum produced the thinkers of the Enlightenment, and in France particularly, the intellectuals established themselves as critics of society by their opposition to the ruling class and to the Church of the *ancien régime*. It is in this role, as critics of society, that the modern intellectuals have frequently been considered.[1] Their part in revolutionary movements, in the labour movement as a whole, and more recently in national liberation movements, has been emphasized in numerous writings, very often in the context of a critique of Marx's theory of the proletarian revolution. One of the earliest writers to present such an account of the influence of intellectuals was a Polish revolutionary, Waclaw Machajski, who set out in a number of books, and especially in *The Intellectual Worker* (1905),[2] the theory that the socialist movement actually expressed the ideology of dissatisfied intellectuals, and that its success would result, not in a classless society, but in the creation of a new ruling class of intellectuals, allied with the new middle class, in a type of society which he called 'state capitalism'. Machajski himself was not entirely pessimistic about the future of socialism, and he considered that through the general improvement of education the predominance of the intellectuals might be diminished and a classless society eventually attained. But his work as a whole received little attention and the idea of the revolutionary intellectuals was taken up in the main by opponents of socialism; originally by Max Nomad, and later by H.D Lasswell, who propounded the view which came to be widely held that most of the revolutions of the twentieth century have been led by intellectuals who succeeded in establishing themselves in power under the banner of socialism.

The role of the intellectuals has been very differently conceived by some other writers. We saw earlier that Mosca regarded the intellectuals as a more or less independent group standing between the bourgeoisie and the proletariat, which might form the nucleus of a new and more worthy élite. In the final pages of his *Sulla Teorica dei governi e sul governo parlamentare* (1884, p. 293) he expresses his hopes thus:

> If there is any social class prepared to set aside, if only for a while, the private interest, and able to perceive the common good with the detachment needed, it is certainly the one which, thanks to its exacting intellectual training, has what should make for nobility of character, for broad horizons and for enlarged faculties . . . that class, and that class alone, will freely sacrifice a present good in order to avert a future evil.

A very similar conception was outlined several decades later by Karl Mannheim (1936, pp. 136–46), who discerned in the 'socially unattached intelligentsia' a relatively classless stratum, recruited from an increasingly inclusive area of social life, bound together by education, and subsuming in itself all those interests with which social life is permeated. Because of these characteristics the intellectuals are capable, according to Mannheim, of acquiring a relatively complete and objective view of their society, and especially of the different interest groups within it, and of acting independently to promote more general social interests.

There is some truth in both the accounts which I have considered. Intellectuals have taken a prominent part in radical and revolutionary movements of various kinds, from the eighteenth century to the present time – against capitalism, colonialism, and military or political dictatorships – but also, on other occasions, in movements supporting capitalism, or even dictatorships. But insofar as many intellectuals were attracted towards the socialist movement from the late nineteenth century this is explicable in other ways than by the theory that they form a new élite which is struggling for power under the deceptive slogans of socialism and the classless society. The labour movement in Western societies was not a simple protest movement. Unlike the sporadic revolts of slaves or peasants who expressed their aspirations largely in the religious imagery which they found ready to hand, it involved, almost from the beginning, a theory of society, in the elaboration of which intellectuals necessarily had an important role. They were attracted to the socialist movement because they found there a place of honour, and also, in some degree, an ideal of social organization which had some of the characteristics – rationality, impartiality and even other-worldliness – which are vital to intellectual life itself. Another factor which was equally important, and perhaps more important, was the social origins of the intellectuals. In many modern societies the universities, and intellectual occupations in general, have constituted one of the principal avenues by which talented individuals from the lower strata of society could rise to more important positions. As a result the social composition of the intellectual élite has usually differed considerably from that of other élites, and it has always been likely that many intellectuals – at least in certain periods – would give their allegiance to the working-class movement.

This view suggests that the intellectual élite, rather than having its own occupational interests or constituting a detached and independent social group, will be associated with, and divided in its allegiance between, major social classes. The second view, according to which the intellectuals do form a group which is capable of taking an objective view of society and of defending consistently some general interest of society as a whole, sets the intellectual élite above classes altogether while still denying that intellectuals are likely to develop a specific group interest of their own.

Neither of these accounts, however, does justice to the diversity and mutability of the situation of intellectuals in modern societies. In the first place, there are important national differences among the industrial countries of Europe and North America. As Aron (1957) observed, French intellectuals tend to have higher social prestige, to be less closely associated with the administrative and practical aspects of political life, and to be more radical critics of their society, than is the case with intellectuals in Britain, Germany or the USA. A study of members of the French Chamber of Deputies from 1871 to 1958 showed that more than half of the 6,000 deputies elected during that period were intellectuals in a broad sense – writers, university teachers, lawyers, journalists, scientists, engineers, school-teachers – and concluded that:

In France, at least, it was the intellectuals who most impassioned political debates in the Assembly under the Fourth Republic, as under the Third. They were very often the most intransigent ideologues. Their 'minds were similarly furnished' in the sense that they were apt to pose problems abstractly, with more or less sincerity, and often to expound them with ability. But this aptitude meant that they often proposed unrealistic solutions; and that they fixed upon subtleties and neglected essentials, thus uselessly complicating and prolonging parliamentary debates by inventing false problems and disagreeing among themselves.

(Dogan 1961, p. 67)

It is interesting to observe, also, from a study of the 'great men' of France (Girard 1961, pp. 239–40), as recorded in the *Petit Larousse*, how prominently intellectuals in the most exclusive sense – writers, artists and scholars – figure in the list, and thus how great their social prestige is considered to be; over several centuries they form by far the largest group, accounting for nearly half the total, and their pre-eminence steadily increased up to the end of the nineteenth century (the latest period covered by the study).[3] In Britain, intellectuals have not possessed such great social prestige as in France, nor have they been so prominent in political life, either by membership of parliament, or by any collective activity of social thought and criticism. Only on rare occasions have groups of intellectuals attracted any considerable public attention, or seemed to have a direct political influence; among the more obvious instances over the past century and a half being the Utilitarian philosophers, the Christian socialists, the early Fabians, those intellectuals who were associated with the Left Book Club and the anti-Fascist organizations of the 1930s, various groups associated with the radical movements of the late 1960s, and in the 1980s notably the groups of right-wing intellectuals in such organizations as the Adam Smith Institute.

This last phenomenon indicates a second important characteristic of the intellectual élite, in most countries and at most times: namely that it is one of the least homogeneous or cohesive of élites, and displays a large diversity of opinion on cultural and political questions. By no means all intellectuals belong or have belonged politically to the left, and for most of the twentieth century it is probably the case that a majority of intellectuals in the West European countries and in the USA have inclined towards the right. There is much evidence that the political attitudes of intellectuals are influenced very strongly by their social class origins; for example, there was a striking difference in France between the students of the former *École libre des Sciences politiques*, recruited almost entirely from the upper class and strongly right-wing in their attitudes, and the students of the *École Normale*, recruited much more widely from the middle class, working class and peasantry, and predominantly left-wing in their attitudes. What is not at all clear, however, is whether intellectuals are less influenced than are other élites by their social class origins, because of the nature of their activities and way of life. Again, there are important historical fluctuations in the social attitudes of intellectuals, which are brought about by more general changes in society. In the 1930s many prominent intellectuals, in Europe and elsewhere, were supporters of the political left; but in the 1950s there was a movement towards the right, and then, after a revival of left-wing thought in the 1960s, an increasing predominance of right-wing ideas again in the 1980s. These fluctuations may be accounted for either by changes in socio-political conditions, and the varying fortunes of different classes and regimes, or by changes in the character of the intellectual élite itself; but at all events they appear to be a regular feature of intellectual and cultural life.

In this context, two features of the recent history of intellectuals in the industrial societies need to be considered. The size and the internal differentiation of the intellectual stratum have both increased, with the expansion of university education and the growth of scientific, technical and professional occupations. At the same time, changes have occurred in the relative importance of different groups within the intellectual élite; experts of one sort or another have come to predominate over the more literary and philosophical exponents of general cultural or social ideas. The growing social importance of natural scientists is clearly to be seen in the amount of public attention which their activities and needs attract, as well as in the emphasis on their role in the shaping of public policy, and more generally on the imperatives of the new 'scientific-technological' revolution. It may be as a consequence of these develop-ments that intellectuals have tended to become less radical critics of society as a whole and to be more concerned with solving the kind of short-term, specific problems which arise out of the complex activities of the industrial societies in which they live. In this sense, the influence of intellectuals has increased in one of the directions which Mosca expected; but the very fact that they are increasingly engaged in such circumscribed, expert tasks makes them less qualified for the position of a ruling élite, because they lack any distinctive group organization or ideology.

A second group which has attracted attention as a potential ruling élite is that constituted by the managers of industry. For a time, the rise of the managers in modern society became a focal point of sociological controversy, largely under the influence of James Burnham's (1943) theory of the managerial revolution, the basic idea of which had been stated much earlier by Veblen (1921). Veblen argued that capitalism, i.e. a system of production directed mainly by the owners of the means of production, could not last, because of its inefficient use of industrial resources, but he did not accept the Marxist view that its downfall would be brought about by the working class, or that it would be followed by a socialist society. He saw the principal opposition to capitalist industry in the technological specialists – the 'engineers' – upon whose work the operation of modern industry depends, and who are in a position, as he claims, to make the next move:

> They are, by force of circumstance, the keepers of the community's material welfare; although they have hitherto been acting, in effect, as keepers and providers of free income for the kept classes. They are thrown into the position of responsible directors of the industrial system, and by the same move they are in a position to become arbiters of the community's material welfare. They are becoming class-conscious, and they are no longer driven by a commercial interest, in any such degree as will make them a vested interest in that commercial sense in which the syndicated owners and the federated workmen are vested interests. They are, at the same time, numerically and by habitual outlook, no such heterogeneous and unwieldy body as the federated workmen, whose numbers and scattering interest has left all their endeavours substantially nugatory.
>
> (ibid., p. 74)

Burnham's thesis was essentially similar, but it was set out in a more elaborate form. He argued that we are living in a period of transition from one type of society to another, from capitalist society (i.e. a society characterized by a particular mode of production, by the dominance of industrialists and bankers, and by specific systems of belief or ideologies) to a type of society which he proposed to call the 'managerial society'. Before explaining the process of transition to this society – the 'managerial revolution' – he discusses the principal alternative theory of the decline of capitalism, the Marxist theory of proletarian revolution. His criticism follows familiar lines: first, that the Russian Revolution did not inaugurate a socialist society, and secondly, that in most of the advanced industrial countries there have been no proletarian revolutions, while in the few cases where they were attempted they were unsuccessful (e.g. Germany in 1918–19). His own theory involves first of all a statement of who are the managers, and then a demonstration that the group which he has defined is in fact becoming a ruling élite in society. Burnham identified two principal sections among the managers: the scientists and technologists, and the directors and co-ordinators of the process of production. The latter are the managers *par excellence*, and he distinguished them from the 'engineers' in Veblen's sense, even though many of them may have scientific or technical qualifications. They are, in fact, the top executives or company directors of business corporations, and Burnham's analysis of their position in society depends in large measure upon establishing that there has developed in modern industrial societies a radical separation between the ownership and the control of industry. The idea of such a separation was familiar to nineteenth-century students of society (including Marx, who observed the consequences of the development of joint stock companies); but its significance has increased with the appearance of the modern giant corporation, which was first systematically examined by Berle and Means (1933). Burnham's argument is that the managers are taking over the economic power which was formerly in the hands of the capitalist owners of industry, and are thus acquiring the capacity to shape the whole social system. He supports his thesis – which requires not only that the managers shall be a distinct social group, but that they shall be a cohesive group, aware of their group interests in a struggle for power – by attempting to show that the individualistic ideology of capitalism is being replaced by a managerialist ideology. As evidence for the latter point he presents the experiences of the Fascist corporate state in Germany and Italy, and of the Communist regime in the Soviet Union (none of which have survived), and the limited amount of state planning in some Western capitalist countries.

Subsequent criticism has made it clear that the fundamental notion of the separation of ownership and control in modern industry is at best a half truth. There is a close connexion between the owners and the managers of industry in several respects. In the first place, the top managers are very often owners, in the sense that they have substantial shareholdings in their companies; and although shareholding may be quite widely dispersed this only makes it easier for a small number of large shareholders to control the policies of the company (Florence 1953). Secondly, even when managers are not important shareholders in their own companies, they are usually wealthy individuals; as Mills (1956, p. 119) pointed out: 'the chief executives and the very rich are *not* two distinct and clearly segregated groups. They are both very much mixed up in the corporate world of property and privilege.' Thirdly, the recruitment of managers is predominantly from the upper strata of society. In the USA, according to Mills, 'the top executives of 1950 are not country boys who have made good in the city', nor are they immigrants or even sons of immigrants; 'these urban, white, Protestant Americans were born into families of the upper and upper middle classes. Their fathers were mainly entrepreneurs: 57 per cent are sons of business men; 14 per cent of professional men; 15 per cent of farmers' (ibid., p. 127).

This conclusion is confirmed by several other studies. William Miller (1962) showed, in a careful investigation of the social origins of 190 prominent American business leaders in the first decade of the present century, that already at that time the notion that the typical successful businessman had risen from the lowest strata of society was obsolete. Less than 10 per cent of those he studied were born abroad, and only 1 per cent could be regarded as 'poor immigrants'. Most of them came from old-established American families, in the larger towns and cities; and 80 per cent of them were from business or professional families. Similarly, a very thorough study of the upper class and the business élite in Philadelphia in 1940 (Baltzell 1962) concluded that the upper class contributed considerably more than its share of leaders within the business community: 75 per cent of the bankers, 51 per cent of the lawyers, 45 per cent of the engineers, and 42 per cent of the business men listed in *Who's Who* were also members of the upper class (i.e. belonged to families listed in the *Social Register*). In addition, of the 532 directorships in industrial and financial institutions reported by members of the élite, 60 per cent were reported by members of the upper class. Finally, the leading bankers and lawyers in the city were members of the upper class. The presidents, and over 80 per cent of the directors in the six largest banks were Proper Philadelphians, as were the senior partners in the largest law firms.

(p. 431)

In Britain a survey of directors of large public companies (Copeman 1955) showed that between 50 and 60 per cent began their careers with the advantage of having business connexions in the family, while another 40 per cent came from families of landowners, professional men and others of similar social level.

More recent research indicates that this situation has not changed significantly over the past few decades. In a series of studies Scott (1979, 1982, 1991) has demonstrated the great concentration of family wealth in Britain, and its connection with the ownership and control of corporate property. With the growth of large corporations the structure of ownership has become more impersonal than it was in the days of the individual entrepreneur, but as Scott (1979, pp. 175–6) argues,

this has not resulted in a loss of power by wealthy persons . . . Wealthy families hold shares in a large number of companies and they form a pool from which corporate managers are recruited, though these managers may not come from families having a substantial ownership stake in the companies which they run. The propertied class has interests throughout the corporate system.

Scott also refers to the increasing importance of educational diplomas, as do Abercrombie and Urry (1983), who relate this, however, to the growth of a 'service class' which in their view is

taking on and concentrating within itself the functions of capital, namely, conceptualization, control, and reproduction, while the class position of the capitalist class is being transformed . . . The process of class formation . . . is increasingly the outcome of the distribution of hierarchically ordered educational credentials.

(p. 153)

But the kind of analysis undertaken by Scott and others, in Britain and in other major industrial countries, shows that private wealth is still dominant in the class structure of these societies. The top executives and the owners of property are so intimately connected as to form a single social group, while the position of those in the middle and lower levels of management (the 'service class') differs fundamentally in that although they play an important part in the organization, technical operation, and administration of many vital economic enterprises and services (also in the public sector) they have, nevertheless, a subaltern role and do not make the crucial strategic decisions about the use of capital. In all this there is little to suggest an imminent 'managerial revolution', or to give verisimilitude to Burnham's sketch of the new managerial ideology. The managers, especially the top managers, form an important functional group in industrial societies; they are an élite in the sense that they have high prestige and make some important economic decisions, and that they are increasingly aware of their position as a functional group (this awareness being fostered by the development of systematic studies and training in management), but they are not independent of the upper class of property owners, and they are not becoming a new and distinctive 'ruling class'.[4]

We have now to consider a third social group – that of the high government officials – which has appeared to many observers as constituting an increasingly powerful élite in modern societies. The concern of sociologists with the bureaucratic élite originated mainly in the work of Max Weber, in the course of his long 'debate with the ghost of Karl Marx' and with Marx's followers. Weber's opposition to socialism was inspired partly by a fear that it would result in the loss of individual freedom and in a more or less total regimentation of social life. Where Marx saw in the history of modern societies a concentration of the means of production in the hands of a small capitalist class, whose dispossession by the working class would be the initial step towards inaugurating a period of increasing human liberty, Weber (1919) saw a process of concentration of the means of administration which would reach its apogee in a socialist society, with the direst consequences for the individual:

> the development of the modern state is initiated through the action of the prince. He paves the way for the expropriation of the autonomous and 'private' bearers of executive power who stand beside him, of those who in their own right possess the means of administration, warfare and financial organization . . . The whole process is a complete parallel to the development of the capitalist enterprise through gradual expropriation of the independent producers. In the end, the modern state controls the total means of political organization.
>
> (p. 82)

Weber did not believe that the power of bureaucracy could be checked by political authorities, even in a democratic system:

> Under normal conditions the power position of a fully developed bureaucracy is always overwhelming. The 'political master' finds himself in the position of the 'dilettante' who stands opposite the 'expert', facing the trained official who stands within the management of administration. This holds whether the 'master' whom the bureaucracy serves is a 'people', equipped with the weapons of 'legislative initiative', the 'referendum', and the right to remove officials, or a parliament, elected on a more aristocratic or more democratic basis and equipped with the right to vote a lack of confidence.
>
> (1921, p. 232)

There can be little doubt that Weber's interpretation was unduly influenced by the example of the Prussian bureaucracy, and its usurpation of political functions in Imperial Germany. Nevertheless, it has also seemed to other scholars that his thesis of the increasing power of bureaucracy gained plausibility from the events of European history in the twentieth century; from the developments which followed the socialist revolution in Russia, and from the consequences of the more extensive control of economic activity by the state in democratic capitalist countries. The application of Weber's ideas to the Soviet social system was made most fully and explicitly by a Yugoslav critic of totalitarian Communism, Milovan Djilas (1957), who refers to 'This new class, the bureaucracy, or more accurately the political bureaucracy', which, he says, has all the characteristics of earlier ruling classes as well as some new characteristics of its own. The new class is 'made up of those who have special privileges and economic preference because of the administrative monopoly they hold'. But Djilas has to admit that its members are not government officials or administrators in the ordinary sense:

> a more detailed analysis will show that only a special stratum of bureaucrats, those who are not administrative officials, make up the core of the governing bureaucracy [or new class]. This is actually a party or political bureaucracy. Other officials are only the apparatus under the control of the new class.

Eventually he has to concede that 'the party makes the class', but he attempts to avoid the consequences of this statement by saying that the class then 'grows as a result and uses the party as a basis. The class grows stronger, while the party grows weaker'. Finally, he attempts to bring the phenomenon within the scope of Marxist theory by asserting that the new class is defined by its ownership of the means of production: 'the proof that it is a special class lies in its ownership and its special relations to other classes . . . The Communist political bureaucracy uses, enjoys, and disposes of nationalized property' (ibid., pp. 39–40).

In my view, this is a somewhat misleading analysis of the élites as they existed in Soviet society. As Djilas himself admits, the new class is not a bureaucracy in the strict sense, because it is not made up of government officials and administrators; in fact, it is not a bureaucracy at all, since those who compose it – the leading party members – are not bureaucrats, any more than the managers of industry are bureaucrats.[5] They are political leaders who rise to power in the party by the exercise of political abilities – tactical skill, cunning, persuasiveness, energy, perseverance and so on – not by passing examinations in Marxism-Leninism.[6] Similarly, the dominance which the party itself exercises is political, not bureaucratic. Djilas really admits this when he says that 'the party makes the [new] class', but he tries to soften the force of the statement by adding that subsequently the class grows stronger at the expense of the party. There is little evidence, however, that the Communist Party in any

Communist country did grow weaker in this particular way, and what Djilas mainly succeeds in expressing is a moral evaluation, an assertion of the decline of the ideal party, the revolutionary proletarian party. Lastly, it is a mistake to suppose that the party ruled because it controlled the means of production; on the contrary, it controlled the means of production because it had political power. As a Polish sociologist argued more generally:

> the nineteenth century conception of social class, in both the liberal and the Marxian interpretations, has lost much of its applicability in the modern world. In situations where changes of social structure are to a greater or lesser degree governed by the decision of the political authorities, we are a long way from . . . classes conceived of as groups determined by their relations to the means of production or, as others would say, by their relations to the market . . . In situations where the political authorities can overtly and effectively change the class structure; where the privileges that are most essential for social status, including that of a higher share in the national income, are conferred by a decision of the political authorities; where a large part or even the majority of the population is included in a stratification of the type to be found in a bureaucratic hierarchy – the nineteenth-century concept of class becomes more or less an anachronism, and class conflicts give way to other forms of social antagonism.
>
> (Ossowski 1963, p. 184)

This makes clear that, while the lower levels of the social hierarchy may be bureaucratically organized, the ruling group itself is a political authority.

I do not wish to suggest that the high state officials were without influence in the USSR and other communist countries; only that they were not a ruling class or governing élite. Even in the Stalinist period, the ruling party had obviously to take some account of the attitudes and aspirations of the various élite groups, including the officials; and in the later more liberal regimes it is evident that high officials, industrial managers, intellectuals and others had some independent influence upon social policies, though this was always severely limited by the surveillance and control exercised by the party.

Does the situation of officials in the Western democracies differ at all from the foregoing? Many writers have drawn attention to what they regard as the increasing power of bureaucracy, which they explain by the increase in the range of activities undertaken by the state, and by the growing complexity of public administration. A critic of the French administrative élite described this situation in the following terms: 'They [the high officials] constitute a supreme and sovereign self-recruiting body, immune from political intervention, a rock against which all political storms beat ineffectively and in vain' (Lüthy 1955, p. 17); while another writer, considering the progress of a 'managerial revolution' in France, observed that

two groups of experts are tending to assume a leading position in the state as in the economy. The élite of the administration is recruited essentially among the *Inspecteurs des finances* and the members of the *Conseil d'État*; it is a general staff which radiates everywhere. Since these administrators frequently transfer to the private sector, they are to be found in the banks and in large-scale industrial and commercial enterprises. The second source is the graduates of the *École polytechnique*, who form the élite of the technical departments of state, but are also increasingly the managers of large-scale industry.

(Siegfried 1957, p. 246)

Such arguments were most common in France in the 1950s, since the power of a bureaucracy always stands out most clearly when the political authority itself is weak or unstable, but they are encountered in all the Western countries in one form or another. Sometimes, as in the work by Siegfried quoted above, the argument is connected with the general thesis of the 'managerial revolution', and it is suggested that the managers of private industry and of nationalized undertakings, and the high government officials, are together developing into a ruling élite. This idea is supported by the observation that there is a growing interchange of personnel between these different sectors of management and adminis-tration. I have shown earlier that the managers do not constitute an independent power élite, and a similar demonstration can be made in the case of officials. Their policy-making powers, however much they may have increased, are ultimately subject to the control of a political authority, and the rivalry between political parties in the democratic countries is one of the means by which this control is made effective. Another means is what we may term the ethical code of the bureaucracy itself, and particularly the doctrine of political neutrality; in many Western countries this doctrine exerts a restraining influence upon any ambition of high officials to usurp the policy-making powers of political leaders.

Furthermore, in the case of officials, as in the case of industrial managers, it is evident from a number of studies that they are closely associated with the upper class in society; and insofar as they do directly influence public policy it is more likely to be along the lines of class interest than along the lines of their own particular aims as a rising élite of power. In Britain, a study by Kelsall (1955) showed that while the social area of recruitment to the administrative class of the higher civil service broadened between 1929 and 1950, there were still very few recruits from the lower strata of the working class (semi-skilled and unskilled workers) which comprise some 30 per cent of the total population; and on the other hand, 30 per cent of the higher civil servants came from families of property owners and professional people which account for only 3 per cent of the population. My own study of the French higher civil service (Bottomore 1952) indicated an even greater bias in recruitment: at the top level, in the *grands corps de l'État*, 84 per cent of the officials came from upper and upper middle-class families, and less than 1 per cent from the families of industrial workers or agricultural labourers. Moreover, both in Britain and in France, higher civil servants have for the most part been educated in prestigious and socially exclusive schools and institutions of higher education, and in this way the social opinions and political outlook of the upper class are perpetuated and reinforced. In France, the *École libre des Sciences politiques* had a particularly important role, up to 1945, in the formation of an administrative élite within the upper class. Its founder, Émile Boutmy, expressed himself clearly on the subject:

> Privilege has gone, democracy cannot be halted. The higher classes, as they call themselves, are obliged to acknowledge the right of the majority, and they can only maintain their political dominance by invoking the right of the most capable. Behind the crumbling ramparts of their prerogatives and of tradition the tide of democracy must encounter a second line of defence, constructed of manifest and useful abilities, of superior qualities whose prestige cannot be gainsaid.
>
> (letter of 25 February 1871)

The postwar reforms of recruitment to the French higher civil service, including the establishment of the *École Nationale d'Administration*, changed to some extent the ethos of education for the administrative élite, making it more 'managerial' and less 'upper class', but they did not bring about major changes in the social area of recruitment. In the USA, on the other hand, the absence of a comprehensive career civil service, especially in the higher grades, has prevented the formation of an administrative élite, and at the same time has made it of less concern to upper-class families to place some of their members in the administration.[7] Mills (1956, pp. 239–41) came to the view that the absence of a genuine bureaucracy was an important factor in allowing the creation of an irresponsible power élite in American society:

> The United States has never and does not now have a civil service, in the fundamental genuine sense of a reliable civil service career, or of an independent bureaucracy effectively above political party pressure ... neither executives nor politicians really want a group of expert administrators who are genuinely independent of party considerations, and who, by training and experience, are the depository of the kind of skills needed to judge carefully the consequences of alternative policies.

But to argue in this way is to neglect all the experience of the European societies, in which the closest association has existed between the high officials of a genuine bureaucracy and the upper class in society.

This account of three élites which have attained prominence in modern societies suggests a number of interesting conclusions about the relations between élites and classes, and about the circulation of élites. Neither the intellectuals, nor the industrial managers, nor the bureaucrats can be seriously regarded as contenders for the place of the governing élite. None of these groups is sufficiently cohesive or sufficiently independent to be considered in such a light. The intellectuals are the most obviously divided among themselves, but all three groups show their lack of cohesion in the fact that they have not produced any doctrine which would express their specific importance and aims in society. A study of their characteristics brings to light a problem which was cogently stated by Friedrich (1950, pp. 257–8) in a criticism of the élite theories: 'No attempt is made by Pareto to show that the 'élite', as defined by him, possesses a distinct group character', and further, 'both writers [Mosca and Pareto] smuggle in as an unproven assumption or major premise what is the most problematical part of all élite doctrines, . . . that those who play a role in government constitute a coherent group'. In spite of the many difficulties presented by the concept of class, it is a great deal easier to demonstrate the existence of broad class interests in modern democratic societies (with the evidence provided by the formation of distinct organizations, by political ideologies and by voting behaviour) than to show that élite groups such as those I have examined here have any similar collective interests, or a collective 'élite-consciousness'.

The autonomy of these élites is limited, as we have seen, in various ways. They have class affiliations, which may be multiple as in the case of the intellectuals, or single, as is mainly the case with the managers and bureaucrats; and so they must be regarded as in some degree the representatives of social classes. The bureaucrats are controlled directly by political authorities, either by a single party in the various forms of totalitarian regime, or by several alternating parties in the democratic countries. The significance of the increasing influence of these élites seems to be not that each of them is a potential ruling class engaged in a struggle for supreme power, but that insofar as there is competition and conflict among them this may restrict to some extent the power of those who are the rulers of society at any given time. They form, to use Mosca's term, elements of the 'sub-élite' in society.

NOTES

1 See Bottomore (1967), Brym (1980). Schumpeter (1942), in his account of the decline of capitalism, greatly exaggerated the influence of radical intellectuals.

2 His books are in Russian and have not been translated. His ideas were first expounded in English by Max Nomad in *Rebels and Renegades* (1932), from which I take this account.

3 As the editor remarks, it would be interesting to obtain similar material from various countries in order to establish a basis for comparing the prestige and influence of intellectuals in different environments. Unfortunately, a beginning has still to be made, or even envisaged; one elaborate and bulky symposium on the intellectuals, edited by De Huszar (1960), still relies largely upon impressionistic accounts of their social role.

4 See Bottomore and Brym (1989), and in particular the chapter by Marceau which discusses the education of French businessmen (pp. 65–9).

5 Cf. Mills (1956, p. 133):

> The bureaucratic career, properly defined, does not mean merely a climb up, from one level to the next, of a hierarchy of offices. It does involve that, but more importantly, it means the setting up of strict and unilateral qualifications for each office occupied. Usually these qualifications involve both specified formal training and qualifying examinations.

6 A study of the Soviet bureaucracy by Armstrong (1959) presents much the same thesis of rule by a bureaucracy. The author shows, in fact, that there was an increasing emphasis upon the formal training of party officials in special party schools, but he does not show that ascent to the topmost positions of power was dependent upon success in this educational system, i.e. upon formal qualifications, rather than upon success in practical political leadership, which included cultivating the 'right connections'.

7 See Bendix (1949). The recruitment is similar to that in Britain or France insofar as few higher civil servants come from working-class families, but the social composition differs as a whole in being more predominantly middle class and lower middle class. Moreover, the American higher officials had a more diversified educational background, as well as being drawn from a variety of previous occupations.

Chapter 5

Tradition and modernity
Élites in the developing countries

There is no context in which the idea of élites has been invoked more frequently since the Second World War than in discussions of the problems and prospects of the 'developing countries'. This should cause no surprise, for as we have seen already there is a profound association between changes in social structure and the rise and fall of élites. Economic, political, or other changes first bring about modifications in the prestige and power of different social groups, and those groups which are increasing their power then seek to take control of the changes and to press them forward. At the same time, the need for 'charismatic' leaders and élites seems to be most keenly felt wherever complex and difficult social changes are taking place and familiar ways of life are disappearing. In the developing countries, therefore, we have an opportunity to study closely those social forces which are creating new élites, as well as the activities of the élites themselves in the attempted transformation of their societies into modern, economically advanced nations.

Each of these countries has, of course, some unique features and problems arising from its history, its geographical situation and its particular relationships with other nations, which may have a greater or lesser influence upon its development; but there are also many important characteristics which are either common to all the countries, or are to be found in those belonging to a particular type. Leaving aside, for the present purpose, the factors of size and natural resources, we can distinguish four main categories of underdeveloped countries, within each of which there are important similarities of social structure and culture: (i) the African states; (ii) the Arab states of the Middle East and North Africa; (iii) the

Asian states; and (iv) the Latin American states. The countries belonging to the first group have established themselves by means of anti-colonial struggles which profoundly affected their political regimes. They have to face, in addition to the problems of economic development, those of consolidating a national community formed out of tribal groups, whose existence within their frontiers is largely the result of the arbitrary division of Africa among the colonial powers. Among the countries of the second group, a number have been formed by independence struggles against direct colonial rule, but many others have enjoyed political independence for some time and have had chiefly to resist the indirect control of their economic resources by foreign powers. Their political problems are mainly those of breaking down feudal and autocratic systems of government, which are linked with highly inegalitarian and rigid class systems. The third group, that of the Asian countries, is characterized especially by the fact that these are, for the most part, countries of ancient civilization in which traditional social institutions are very strongly established. They are also, in many cases, countries which have liberated themselves very recently from colonial rule, and although they do not confront major problems of integrating tribal groups into a national community, as is the case with the African countries, they face some similar problems of national integration insofar as they are divided into castes or linguistic regions (as in India), or into ethnically and linguistically separate groups (e.g. Tamils and Sinhalese in Sri Lanka, Malays and Chinese in Malaysia). The fourth group, that of the Latin American countries, differs in important respects from all the others. These countries are, for the most part, more advanced economically, and they are already urban rather than agrarian societies, although they have begun to industrialize on a large scale only in the past few decades; and they have been politically independent for a relatively long time. Thus, their political problems are not to the same extent those of national integration, although in some of them, such as Peru, the large Indian population has still to acquire full citizenship; nor has recent political activity been directly inspired by nationalism, although it has been directed increasingly against North American economic influence in the region. The main problems are those created by industrialization, the rapid increase of population, and the rise of a labour movement within a political system in which the large landowners have long been dominant, and have often ruled through military dictatorships.

The general problems of the developing countries arise largely from the accelerated pace of industrialization which is sought, and in varying degrees achieved, and which has been provoked to a considerable extent by the example of those countries which are already industrialized; from the rapid growth of population resulting from the improvement of medical care and other welfare services; and from the social and political conditions in which economic development has to take place. The industrialization of the Western countries began, in most cases, in more favourable conditions of economic organization, political cohesion and stability, and psychological preparation of the population by the decline of traditional institutions, as well as being a more protracted and gradual process. Quite apart from the economic difficulties which the present developing countries encounter from the fact that there are already in the world advanced industrial countries, which dominate world production, trade and investment, they have also to contend with political instability, with popular demands for rapid improvement in levels of consumption and welfare, and sometimes with powerful opposing forces based upon traditional ways of life.

In such conditions the importance of élites and leaders who are capable of inspiring effective action, of controlling and directing events, is greatly enhanced. It is further enhanced by the lack of experience in social and political organization of the mass of the population who have in many cases been kept in a condition of subjection and inactivity by autocratic rulers, either indigenous or foreign. Which, then, are the new élites that emerge to initiate or to take over the tasks of economic development and social reconstruction? How are they related to social classes and how effective is their leadership? One early study of industrial society and industrialization suggested that 'there are five ideal types of élites who customarily and variously take the leadership of the industrialization process . . . (1) a dynastic élite; (2) the middle class; (3) the revolutionary intellectuals; (4) the colonial administrators; and (5) the nationalist leaders' (Kerr *et al.* 1960, especially chap. 3). Two of these élites have been relatively unimportant in the most recent period and we can deal with their influence very briefly. The colonial administrators created, in many countries of Asia and Africa, some of the prerequisites for industrial development, by establishing an effective administration and judiciary, introducing modern education, and promoting modern banking and commerce, as well as some modern industries.[1] Nevertheless, these achievements could not lead directly to rapid industrialization, for a number of reasons: the economic interests of the colonial power and the generally inhibiting effects of foreign rule were both serious obstacles, as was the fact that where large-scale commerce and industry did develop it was very often in the hands of nationals of the colonial power.

The role of dynastic élites – whether drawn from a landowning or a commercial aristocracy – is also limited. In some countries of the Middle East and Latin America élites of this kind have attempted, sometimes under foreign as well as internal pressure, to bring about social and economic changes from above, but their actions are constrained by the interest which they have as a class in maintaining the existing state of society. In order to carry out successfully their policies of reform they would have to permit, and still more encourage, much greater social mobility, to extend education rapidly, and to make their own élite positions more easily accessible to individuals and groups from the lower strata of society. It is doubtful whether they can or will do this on the scale or with the speed necessary to meet the urgent demands for economic growth and rising levels of living, and to counter the influence of the new élites emerging from the labour movement which are competing with them for support.

The other three élites which I have mentioned play a more significant role in most of the underdeveloped countries. The middle class as a whole influences economic development not only by the contribution of its special skills, but by a general commitment to modern ways of living. In the various types of developing society, different groups within the middle class may have a more or less predominant influence. In most of the former colonial countries of Asia and Africa the middle class was created largely by the educational and administrative systems which the ruling colonial powers introduced, as may be seen particularly clearly in the case of India. An Indian historian, B.B. Misra (1961), in his well-documented account of the growth of the middle class there, has observed that 'the bulk of the Indian middle classes came to consist of the intelligentsia – public servants, other salaried employees, and members of the learned professions' (p. 343). One important reason for this pre-eminence of the intelligentsia in the middle class was the lack of opportunities for the formation of an indigenous business class, which in turn was due to the low rate of economic growth and to the privileged position of nationals of the colonial power in the small sector of modern industry and commerce. This situation was not affected significantly at first – or even later in the case of those countries which embarked on a socialist path of development – by political independence, because the planning of economic growth and the concentration of effort upon public rather than private enterprise offered relatively little scope for the development of an influential entrepreneurial group. On the other hand, in the countries of Latin America and the Middle East entrepreneurs emerged much earlier, and they formed an important section of the middle class. In the Middle East the development of the oil industry has created massive corporate wealth, though much of this is in the hands of dynastic élites, and extensive industrialization and modernization; but in Latin America, while corporate wealth has also increased, the dominant élites have not been conspicuously effective in promoting sustained economic growth, and there has been since 1958 a succession of economic crises along with increasing problems of foreign indebtedness. This, together with the association between Latin American business and the North American firms which have a large share in the raw materials and other industries, and have ruthlessly exploited natural resources and exported the profits, has tended to discredit the indigenous entrepreneurial élite. The opposition to its rule, and to the activities of North American business interests, was strengthened by the Cuban revolution, and subsequently by the advent of the Popular Unity government in Chile and of the Sandinista government in Nicaragua. From the 1960s new élites, based upon the working class and peasantry, developed rapidly throughout Latin America, but powerful counter-revolutionary movements then emerged, involving military leaders and supported in various ways by the USA, and during the 1980s the advance of the democratic and socialist movements was, at least temporarily, halted.

Within the 'white-collar' middle class in many developing countries one of the most important groups has been that formed by the higher government officials, who assumed exceptional responsibilities and acquired considerable powers, especially in those countries where economic and social planning was undertaken on a large scale. In many respects, government officials seemed to have a role in the economic development of new nations in the twentieth century similar to that which capitalist entrepreneurs had performed in the economic development of Western societies in the eighteenth and nineteenth centuries. But for all their importance their power is more closely circumscribed. The capitalist entrepreneurs were an independent class whose influence spread through government and administration, while the officials are the subordinates of political leaders, constrained by the aims of the governing élite and of the class which sustains it; and a managerial or bureaucratic revolution is no more evident in the developing countries than it is in the advanced industrial societies.

It is the political élite which has been pre-eminent in deciding the course of economic and social development. The origins of this élite are to be found, in most cases, in one or other of the two groups mentioned earlier – the nationalist leaders, and what Kerr *et al.* (1960) called 'revolutionary intellectuals', though it would be more appropriate to refer to them as leaders of revolutionary, radical or labour parties and move- ments – which in some cases are associated or merge with one another. In most of the Asian and African countries, however, intellectuals did take a prominent part in the struggles against colonial rule. University students were often the shock troops of the independence movements, and those who studied abroad created or helped to create the new nationalist parties. A study of the new Indonesian élites (Van Niel 1960), dealing with the early phases of an independence movement, noted the spread of radical ideas among university students and the strong influence of politically minded intellectuals, and showed that educated Indonesians formed a majority of the active participants in the anti-colonial movements. In Nigeria, a new élite of 'Western-educated and frequently self-made men' supplanted the old élite of the traditional ruling families as the independence movement developed, although, as in most cases, there was some overlapping between the old and new élites, since the old élite families were those which had the best opportunities to procure a Western education for their children (Smythe and Smythe 1960). Hodgkin (1961) also pointed out, in his study of African political parties, that nationalistic political élites were recruited very largely from the new middle class, and especially from the 'educated middle class'. In the Ghana House of Assembly, after the 1954 election, 29 per cent of the members were school teachers, 17 per cent clerks, accountants, etc.,

17 per cent members of the liberal professions. Among members of the Legislative Assembly of the eight territories of the former French West Africa, after the 1957 elections, 22 per cent were teachers, 27 per cent were government officials and 20 per cent were members of the liberal professions (ibid., p. 29).

But nationalist leaders have not always been either intellectuals or revolutionaries. In India, they were neither the one nor the other. True, the National Congress was largely created, and was strongly influenced in its early stages, by intellectuals who had imbibed Western ideas; but they were liberals, not revolutionaries, and their influence was later counteracted by that of political leaders who came from business communities or the professions, and even more by the moral and social doctrines of Gandhi, which were derived from traditional religious thought.

Where revolutionary intellectuals did attain power it was usually through the adoption of Marxism as a political creed, and by the formation of Communist parties or similar organizations which brought them into a close association with the industrial workers and especially with the poorer peasants. The initial appeal of Marxism and Communism in the developing countries was well stated by Raymond Aron (1950, p. 154):

> communism may be a progressive force wherever élites are inadequate for their task, either preserving a more or less feudal system of organization, or proceeding too slowly with the capitalist equipment of the country ... In our day an élite which fails to make use of technical resources to raise the standard of life and increase the wealth of the community is indeed a bankrupt élite. It is natural that a party, representative of the peasants and workers, who are in poverty because the productivity of their labour is low, should come forward to take over from the soldiers, bankers or great landowners who prefer to spend their profits on luxurious American cars rather than on tractors or machine tools.

The appeal of Communism was enhanced in the early postwar period by the fact that the Communist parties possessed, in Marxism, an effective 'political formula' (to use Mosca's term[2]) – that is, a doctrine which states clearly the ends to be pursued, and supplies a moral justification of the governing élite and its actions. Marxism was presented as a progressive, modern view of the world, irreconcilably opposed to ancient superstitions; an egalitarian creed which had the power to enthuse individuals everywhere and most of all in those countries where immense wealth and the most degrading poverty coexist; and at the same time a theory of rapid industrialization which incites people to activity and labour and could claim in the economic growth of the USSR up to 1939, and again in the period of postwar reconstruction, a practical confirmation of its truth. Marxism, from this aspect, might be thought of as the 'Protestant ethic' of the twentieth-century industrial revolutions. Nevertheless, as we have seen, the intellectuals are by no means everywhere animated by revolutionary ideas, still less by those of Marxism; and economic development has not in most cases been pursued under the leadership of Communist parties. The resistances to Marxism are numerous and they grow both from within Marxist thought itself and from other systems of ideas. As an intellectual scheme, Soviet Marxism generated increasing doubts and criticisms, some of which I have considered in an earlier chapter; but more important in the present context is the fact that its more repellent aspects as a practical creed came to be clearly recognized. The experience of the USSR, which showed on one hand the possibilities of rapid economic growth under the leadership of the Communist Party (at least up to the 1960s), revealed on the other hand, as possible or even probable concomitants of this kind of one-party rule, dictatorship and loss of personal liberty, persecution and widespread suffering. It is for these reasons that so many intellectuals in the developing countries began to look for a new progressive creed, which they hoped to find, at various times, in African or Asian socialism, in the doctrines of the Cuban revolutionaries, or elsewhere, but which still eludes any precise and compelling formulation – still more so after the collapse of the East European Communist regimes.

If we now look at the external influences we can see that in many developing countries Marxism has been opposed both by traditional religious thinkers and by those who have adopted Western conservative or liberal ideas. Thus in India, although the Communist Party – now divided – constituted at the outset a significant opposition to the Congress Party, the general intellectual and political impact of Marxism has been limited, and even the more reformist socialist ideas which had a prominent place in the Congress itself in the first years of independence seem to have lost much of their appeal. In Latin America the influence of Marxism has been stronger, and has notably affected conceptions of development itself, through the elaboration of theories of 'dependent development' (Kay 1991), but the political impact of socialism has come from a wide variety of sources, including 'liberation theology' (McHugh 1991) and ecology movements. Moreover, as in Asia and Africa, socialist doctrines have been strongly contested by other 'Western' ideas, particularly in the 1980s those expounded by advocates of a 'free market' economy. The relative strength of these opposing conceptions is determined to a great extent by the specific form in which the world economy has evolved, and this is a major external factor to which I shall return later.

The leaders of nationalist movements clearly formed one of the most important élite groups in the Asian and African countries, where the impetus for economic development came originally from the struggles for political independence. Such leaders may be the products of Western universities and radical student movements, but also of indigenous business and professional communities, or of traditional élite groups, and all of them derive their power from leadership of a political party which is based upon, and expresses, some kind of nationalist sentiment. This nationalism is a consequence of the struggle for independence from alien rulers, and also of the nature of the problems which confront these countries after independence; especially the need to create or consolidate a nation out of associated but still separate tribal or linguistic groups, and to plan on a national scale the industrial development of the country. It is not surprising to find, then, that in many developing countries a single party which had successfully led the independence movement established itself as the ruling élite and justified its power both by its past deeds and by its promise to create a modern nation in the future. This is not to say that nationalism is the only 'political formula' which sustains such ruling élites. Other ideas, of democracy, socialism, or welfare, may be incorporated in the ruling doctrine, just as in other cases nationalist ideas may find their place in a revolutionary ideology. In Africa, nationalism was infused with socialistic doctrines on one hand, and with ideas of pan-Africanism, taking shape in actual projects of federation, on the other. Similarly, in many of the Asian countries nationalism had a distinct socialistic cast, and in some countries of the Middle East and Latin America the growth of nationalism was associated with socialism by reason of its opposition to foreign business interests.

One factor, however, which makes nationalism by itself an ambiguous doctrine for the political rulers of developing countries is that it may be backward-looking and seek to revive traditional institutions and traditional élites, especially in those societies which have preserved their own ancient civilization. In the course of the independence movement there may develop, alongside the political struggle, a cultural conflict in which the language, values and institutions of the foreign rulers are rejected while the country's own ancient glories and accomplishments are lauded and held up for imitation. One example of this pattern of events is the revival of Hinduism in India, which was both used and furthered by Gandhi in creating a mass movement of opposition to British rule; but other instances can be found in some Arab countries, in Pakistan, and in some parts of Africa, where Islam provided a rallying point for opponents of colonial rule.[3] Where nationalism is associated in this way with a traditionalist revival of ancient values and ways of life, it may become an obstacle to economic development, especially by its opposition to a thoroughgoing rationalization of social life. Thus, although nationalist political leaders have powerful forces on their side they also confront serious difficulties arising from the conflict between traditionalists and modernists within their own ranks and in the society at large. A further major problem is that where the new nation itself contains different tribal or ethnic groups, or even other distinct nations, profound conflicts may develop from the rise of new independence movements within the nation-state, as has been seen in another context in Eastern Europe since the collapse of the Communist regimes.

There is, finally, an important social group which I have not so far mentioned, but which has been, in some countries, more influential than either the intellectuals or the political leaders: namely, military officers. It is evident that in newly independent countries, where political institutions are still in the making and political authority is still, in varying degrees, unsettled and insecure, those who control the ultimate power of direct physical coercion have the opportunity to play an important part in deciding the future of the nation. Whether they will in fact intervene in political affairs depends upon many factors: the traditions in which military officers have been educated, their social origins, the extent of their influence over the troops they command, and on the other side, the strength of the political leaders and the character of their relations with the military chiefs.[4] Some of the principal examples of military intervention in politics have occurred in Latin America, where they were common in an earlier period when the *caudillos* with their armed bands resembled feudal barons, reacting to the breakdown of a settled political authority (Lieuwen 1961). More recently, however, military intervention has been undertaken primarily in opposition to democratic and socialist movements which threaten the position of the upper class, and although the broad democratic movement has become stronger in some countries it is still not entirely secure, while the socialist movement appears to face a permanent danger of intervention. Elsewhere, there are many other factors to be considered which may enhance the importance of the military. Pye (1961, p. 83) noted that they had become the dominant group in at least eight of the African and Asian countries, and suggested that the political role of the army in the developing countries should be considered

> first, with respect to the political implications of the army as a modern institution that has been somewhat artificially introduced into disorganized transitional societies: and second, with respect to the role that such an army can play in shaping attitudes towards modernity in other spheres of society.

Armies, he argued, are among the most modern elements in some developing countries, and are imbued with 'the spirit of rapid technological change'. At the same time, they are an important modernizing influence upon the society at large, for they train their members in modern techniques and inculcate new attitudes to work.

There is another characteristic of these new armies to which a number of writers have drawn attention: namely that they constitute, or did constitute in the early period of independence, one of the most effective channels of upward social mobility. In those societies in which higher education has been accessible only to the upper class, and in which the political leaders were also drawn largely from this class, the army provided an opportunity for a new élite to form, recruited from the middle strata of society, and sometimes allying itself with the peasantry and working class. In Egypt, Syria and Iraq, revolutions were led by young army officers who belonged in the main to the middle class and lower middle class. In Latin America, too, military intervention in politics sometimes took a different form during the 1930s and 1940s, in popular revolutions led by the young officers,[5] but as I have indicated the pattern has changed radically again in the postwar period.

This short review of élite groups in the developing countries – intellectuals, leaders of political movements, an established upper class, military officers, bureaucrats, business leaders – poses the question of how particular élites are able to attain power and to take a leading role in development. Let us consider first some of the internal factors. In some cases, in Latin America and the Middle East, dynastic élites constituted by landowners or royal households, and more recently by entrepreneurs, are strongly established and difficult to dislodge, even where their rule is ineffective or directly impedes economic growth. Military intervention may be favoured in some countries by a tradition of military rule, as in much of Latin America, or by a cultural tradition which does not emphasize the separation of military and political functions, as may be the case in Islamic countries; or on the other hand it may be discouraged by a strongly established doctrine of military neutrality and subordination to civil authority, as is most likely in those countries whose colonial rulers were themselves committed to such a doctrine. Other important factors are the strength of nationalist movements or labour movements, and the ability of their leaders to maintain popular support for their policies. Such support, if the imposition of autocratic control backed by military force is to be avoided, is essential in conditions where development is a more deliberate and conscious process than it was in the first industrial revolution, and is driven partly by popular aspirations for living standards comparable with those in the industrialized countries.

But the internal factors I have considered – the competence of traditional élites and their control of resources (including military force), the political orientations of intellectuals and military officers, the growth of the middle class and of an entrepreneurial stratum, the influence of government officials in directing the economy, the ability of new political movements and leaders to gain mass support – although they play an important part in deciding the course of development and its degree of success, are by no means the only ones to be taken into account, and in many cases not the most crucial. The world economy in the postwar period has been increasingly dominated by capitalism – by giant multinational corporations, by the advanced capitalist nation states (especially until the 1980s by the USA), and by the World Bank and the International Monetary Fund. The relation of these agencies to the developing countries is shaped above all by the interests of capitalism, and the policies of the World Bank and the IMF in particular have contributed massively to the impoverishment of a large part of the Third World (and to the destruction of the natural environment), while at the same time creating or strengthening in these countries small, wealthy, and frequently corrupt élites.[6]

Against this trend the former Soviet bloc was unable to mount any effective resistance, partly because of its relative economic weakness, partly because the regimes of the East European countries comprising it were themselves dominated by a privileged (and also often corrupt) élite. More surprisingly, the democratic socialist governments which were in power at various times in Western Europe seem never to have questioned seriously the policies that were being imposed on the Third World, and it is only since the late 1980s that a more critical attitude has begun to emerge, due largely to the activities of numerous non-governmental organizations and social movements. Nevertheless, in spite of the dominant trend, a number of countries did embark on a socialist path of development, and the achievements and problems of some of them are well analysed in a study by White *et al.* (1983). Since then several of the socialist developing countries have succumbed to outside pressure, and those which survive face many difficulties – in Cuba the relentless, insensate hostility of the USA has been heroically and so far successfully resisted for three decades, but at great cost; in China, notwithstanding the movement towards 'market socialism', and relatively successful continuing economic development, the problems arising from the confrontation between an ageing, autocratic governing élite and popular demands for a more democratic political system; and in a few African countries the economic hardships resulting from the attempt, in very poor societies, to go 'against the stream' – as in Zimbabwe, which is still, however, despite the kind attentions of the IMF, the most successful developing country in southern Africa.

The formation of élites in the developing countries, and the characteristics of those which become dominant, have therefore to be seen as an outcome of the operation of both internal and external factors, with the latter having a pre-eminent influence in much of the Third World. But there is another aspect of this situation which also requires attention. Because of the path that development has taken as a result of Western policies, there are vast and increasing inequalities within the developing countries, an immense gulf between the élites and the mass of the population; and this is very far from the notion of 'democratic élites' expounded by Mannheim and others which I shall examine in the next chapter.

NOTES

1 I mention here the actual achievements of colonial administrators. I do not mean to assert that similar developments could not have taken place indigenously if there had not been colonial conquests, although in many cases this seems to me doubtful.

2 Mosca (1939, p. 70):

> ruling classes do not justify their power exclusively by de facto possession of it, but try to find a moral and legal basis for it, representing it as the logical and necessary consequence of doctrines and beliefs that are generally recognized and accepted . . . This legal and moral basis, or principle, on which the power of the political class rests, is what we have elsewhere called . . . the 'political formula'.

3 For example, a study of Senegal before independence observes that

> the power and influence of the traditional political chiefs has to a large extent been transferred to the Khalifas of the great Islamic sects; the latter represent today the principal force capable of resisting the modernist élite, and one with which the latter and the political movements identified with it must to some extent come to terms

> (Mercier 1956)

4 For a general discussion of the factors involved see Finer (1962, especially chaps 8 and 9), and the comparative study by Janowitz (1964).

5 Lieuwen (1961, p. 132):

> In a number of Latin American countries . . . the pattern of revolution underwent radical change in the second quarter of the twentieth century . . . The general picture was one in which the young officers, also frustrated in their ambitions, made common cause with the rising popular groups. Together they collaborated in bringing down, by force, the *ancien regime*.

The examples given are Bolivia in 1936, Guatemala in 1944, Argentina in 1943 and Colombia in 1953.

6 This process, euphemistically described as 'aid for development', is thoroughly and revealingly analysed in the study by Hancock (1991).

Chapter 6

Democracy and the plurality of élites

The criticism of democratic theories of politics which Mosca and Pareto formulated in the theory of élites began with the observation that in every society there is a minority which effectively rules. This criticism could be met – as Mosca himself saw – while accepting the need for a governing élite in every society, by arguing that the distinctive feature of democracy, as a form of government, is that it permits élites to form freely, and establishes a regulated competition between them for the positions of power. This conception of democracy as a political system in which political parties compete for the votes of a mass electorate implies further that the élites are relatively 'open' and are recruited on the basis of merit (i.e. there is presumed to be a continuous and extensive circulation of élites), and that the whole adult population is able to participate in ruling society at least in the sense that it can exercise a choice between the rival élites. Karl Mannheim, as we saw earlier, had originally connected élite theories with Fascism, and with anti-intellectualist doctrines of 'direct action', but came later to hold a view of this kind:

> the actual shaping of policy is in the hands of élites; but this does not mean that the society is not democratic. For it is sufficient for democracy that the individual citizens, though prevented from taking a direct part in government all the time, have at least the possibility of making their aspirations felt at certain intervals . . . Pareto is right in stressing that political power is always exercised by minorities (élites), and we may also accept Robert Michels' law of the trend towards the oligarchic rule in party organizations. Nevertheless, it would be wrong

to overestimate the stability of such élites in democratic societies, or their ability to wield power in arbitrary ways. In a democracy, the governed can always act to remove their leaders or to force them to take decisions in the interests of the many.

(1956, p. 179)

He also emphasized the importance of selection by merit, and of the reduced distance between élites and masses in creating a compatibility between élite rule and democratic government:

We assume that democracy is characterized, not by the absence of all élite strata, but rather by a new mode of élite selection and a new self-interpretation of the élite ... What changes most of all in the course of democratization is the distance between the élite and the rank-and-file. The democratic élite has a mass background; this is why it can mean something for the mass.

(ibid., p. 200)

The reconciliation between the idea of élites and the idea of democratic government has proceeded apace during the twentieth century, as Mannheim's own work bears witness, and it has been assisted by a number of favourable circumstances. One of these is the general enhancement of the importance of leadership which has resulted from large-scale warfare, from international rivalry in economic growth and from the rise and development of new nations; all of which has tended to divert attention away from the more disagreeable aspects of élite rule towards the need for efficient and enterprising élites. Another circumstance which has lent support to the competition model of democracy is the contrast between the consequences of élite rule in one-party states, and the experiences of those democratic societies in which there is competition for power among several political parties, none of which aims to bring about radical changes in the social structure. Furthermore, this model also has a scientific appeal, by reason of the analogy which it presents to the model of economic behaviour in a free enterprise system, and of the promise which it thus holds out of an analysis of political behaviour as exact and rigorous, if also as limited, as economic analysis. The analogy was stated plainly by Schumpeter (1942, chap. 22), who also went on to argue more generally that modern democracy arose with the capitalist economic system and is causally connected with it (ibid., pp. 296–7). The view is conveyed succinctly in the remark made by a successful politician, which Schumpeter quotes: 'What businessmen do not understand is that exactly as they are dealing in oil so I am dealing in votes' (ibid., p. 285). This conception of democracy as a competition for votes between political parties has been presented in more elaborate forms, as for example in *An Economic Theory of Democracy* by A. Downs, who summarizes his theory in the following way:

> Our main thesis is that parties in democratic politics are analogous to entrepreneurs in a profit-seeking economy. So as to attain their private ends, they formulate whatever policies they believe will gain the most votes, just as entrepreneurs produce whatever products they believe will gain the most profits for the same reasons.
>
> (1957, pp. 295–6)

(See also the critical study of these ideas by Barry [1970]). Another example of the use of this model is to be found in the tentative efforts to apply the theory of games to political behaviour, i.e. to apply to the activities of political parties a mathematical scheme which is extensively used in analysing the behaviour of business enterprises.[1]

But it is not only the competition between political parties which serves to reconcile the existence of élites with democracy. The advocates of this view discover a more general system of checks and balances in the plurality of élites which characterizes democratic societies. Raymond Aron (1950, p. 10) presented the case in a cogent manner:

> although there are everywhere business managers, government officials, trade union secretaries and ministers, they are not everywhere recruited in the same way and they may either form one coherent whole or remain comparatively distinct from one another. The fundamental difference between a society of the Soviet type and one of the Western type is that the former has a unified élite and the latter a divided élite. In the USSR the trade union secretaries, the business managers and the higher officials generally belong to the Communist party ... On the other hand, democratic societies, which I would rather call pluralistic societies, are full of the noise of public strife between the owners of the means of production, trade union

leaders and politicians. As all are entitled to form associations, professional and political organizations abound, each one defending its members' interests with passionate ardour. Government becomes a business of compromises. Those in power are well aware of their precarious position. They are considerate of the opposition because they themselves have been, and will one day again be, in opposition.

The definition of democracy as competition between élites may be criticized on various grounds – that it is excessively arbitrary and leaves out of account generally recognized characteristics of the phenomenon which it defines, or that the theory in which it is used is inadequate or untrue, or that it proceeds from a set of value judgements to which other value judgements can be opposed. Modern democracy has most often, and by most political thinkers, been defined as the participation of the mass of the people in government, and one of its classical formulations is that of Lincoln's Gettysburg Address: 'government of the people, by the people, for the people'. All élite theories deny that there can be, in any real sense, government by the people.[2] The denial may be founded, as in the case of Pareto and Mosca, upon the somewhat trivial observation that in most known societies of the past there has been a clear distinction between the rulers and the ruled, or it may rest upon a more theoretical analysis, as in the writings of Michels, Mannheim and Aron, which attempts to show that in any large and complex society (and in large and complex organizations within society) democracy can only be representative, not direct, and that the representatives are a minority who clearly possess greater political power than those whom they represent, since the influence of the latter is confined to passing judgement, at fairly long intervals, upon the activities of the minority.

But several objections can be brought against this analysis. In the first place, according to the view of democracy which we are now considering, the system of government by representation is quite clearly regarded as an imperfect realization of democracy, to the extent that it does permanently exclude the many from any experience of government. The undemocratic character of representative government becomes most apparent when the representative principle is applied in a system of indirect election, whereby an elected élite itself elects a second élite which is endowed with equal or superior political power. This device has often been resorted to by the opponents of popular rule, and de Tocqueville, among others, saw in it an effective means of restricting democracy. Even when the defenders of the idea of democracy as competition between élites do not propound it deliberately as a defence against democracy in its other sense – against that incursion of the masses into politics which de Tocqueville, Pareto, Mosca and Ortega y Gasset unite in deploring – they are still inclined to take representative government as the ideal, instead of measuring it against the ideal of direct participation by the people in legislation and administration and looking about for means by which this end might be more closely approached.

This argument suggests a second objection to the analysis of democracy which Schumpeter, Aron and others provide. According to their accounts democracy is to be conceived as something accomplished and complete, which can be contrasted straightforwardly with other types of political system. On the other hand, in the conception of democracy as government *by* the people which prevailed during most of the nineteenth century, democracy was conceived as a continuing process in which political rights, the power to influence decisions on social policy, were progressively extended to groups in the population which had formerly been deprived of them. This implies two things: first, that democracy appeared primarily as a doctrine and political movement of the lower classes of society against the dominance of the aristocratic and wealthy classes (and this is, of course, one of the main causes which provoked the response of the élite theories); and secondly, that it was regarded as a movement towards an ideal condition of society in which people would be fully self-governing, which might never be completely achieved, but which democrats ought to strive for. It would not have occurred to most of the democratic political thinkers of the nineteenth century to regard universal suffrage, competition between several political parties and representative government, however valuable by contrast with the institutions of other political regimes, as the ultimate point of democratic progress, beyond which it was impossible to venture.

The reasons for the emergence, in the twentieth century, of a static conception of democracy in which élite rule is sanctioned by periodic elections have to be sought in the political circumstances of this century. It was the establishment of one-party states, in a Fascist form in Germany and Italy, and in a Communist form in the USSR, which gave point and credibility to the identification of democracy with a multi-party, representative system. The passage which I quoted earlier from Aron, in which the unified élite in Soviet-type societies is contrasted with the plurality of élites in Western-type societies, makes this perfectly clear. We may, however, question whether organized political parties – and, more broadly, organized élite groups – are either necessary or sufficient for the existence of a democratic system of government. It has often been held that they are not necessary, and that, for example, in a more decentralized type of political system than those which now exist in most modern nations, the selection of the political leaders for the time being might be accomplished through the activities of associations which would be less highly organized, less bureaucratic and less permanent than the present-day political parties. This view has been taken, notably, by some ecology movements, but where Green parties have been formed in order to contest elections it has proved difficult to avoid more traditional forms of organization within existing political systems.

It may be argued further, however, that in a society from which social classes had been eliminated (which many thinkers have envisaged as a consequence of the growth of democracy) one of the most important bases for the formation of parties would likewise have disappeared; and although it is not impossible to think of other social distinctions which might engender political parties, it is difficult to conceive that such parties would have the same scope and influence in political life, or would be quite so permanent and monolithic, as those with which we are familiar now. This argument refers, it should be noted, to a political system without political parties of the present type, and not to a one-party regime. The latter is not democratic at all, for it deprives the individual, confronted by the ruling party, of any real possibility of expressing or giving effect to his or her disagreement with important social decisions, since there is lacking any forum in the shape of autonomous associations in which alternative opinions can be expounded or the opinions of fellow citizens discovered. It may well be that in periods of popular enthusiasm a single party does express the common purpose of the great majority of a nation, and succeeds in drawing large numbers of people, without compulsion, into the activities of legislation and administration; but in that case there can be no need for it to suppress such other political parties as still survive. It may also be that the rule of a single party, or a coalition, can be justified by the necessities of war, of rapid industrialization, or of the creation of a new nation out of a former colonial territory, but that does not make the political regime in which it functions a democratic one. If the necessity can be demonstrated, the ruling group may be regarded as governing *for* the people, but it is not the case that the people govern themselves.

A discussion of whether political parties are necessary to a democratic system of government must remain unavoidably speculative, and it is both easier and more practical to consider whether the competition between parties and élites is *sufficient* to ensure democracy. There are many liberal thinkers today who would assert that it is sufficient, or who would at least regard the competition between élites as being so important as to absolve them from further enquiry into the conditions of democracy. They would have the support of Mannheim, who, as we have seen, claimed that what made a society democratic was simply that individual citizens should have 'at least the *possibility* of making their aspirations felt at certain intervals'.[3] On the other hand, Schumpeter and Aron both pay much attention to other influences upon the political system. Schumpeter sets out explicitly what he terms 'conditions for the success of the democratic method', which he classifies under four headings: (i) that the human material of politics (i.e. the élites) should be of sufficiently high quality; (ii) that the effective range of political decision should not be extended too far; (iii) that the government should be able to command the services of a well-trained bureaucracy of good standing and tradition; and (iv) that there should be democratic self-control, i.e. that the competing élites should tolerate each other's rule and should resist the offerings of crooks and cranks, while the electorate, having made its choice, should refrain from interfering incessantly in the political actions of its representatives. Similarly, Aron (1950) states three conditions for the success of the contemporary pluralistic democracies: (i) the restoration of government authority capable of settling the disputes between groups and enforcing the decisions necessary in the community's joint interest; (ii) an efficient economic administration which will preserve mobility and revive incentives; and (iii) a limitation of the influence of those individuals and groups which want to change the whole framework of society.

It is obvious, however, that these accounts remain within the scheme of ideas which sees democracy as competition between élites, and explore its further implications, while they neglect many other factors which influence the success or failure, and the extent, of democracy in a larger sense. I shall examine first some of the other political influences. It has been very generally assumed – it is assumed, for example, by Mannheim, although this does not accord well with his other pronouncements on the conditions for democracy – that the development of a democratic polity requires, in addition to the competition between élites, changes in the structure and composition of élites, in their self-conceptions, and in their relations with the rest of the population. Briefly, it seems to be assumed that in a democracy there will be a more rapid and extensive movement of individuals into and out of the élites, that there will be an increasing number of élite positions in relation to the population as a whole, that the élites will develop a less 'aristocratic' outlook and will regard themselves as being closely linked with the masses, and that, in consequence of various levelling influences, they will actually be closer to the masses in their style of life. The first two of these conditions would bring about a situation in which a far greater number of individuals had the experience of ruling as well as of being ruled, while the other conditions would change the character of political rule in some measure, making it less remote, authoritarian, majestic and irresistible. If we now look at the Western democracies of the present day we shall see that, while they conform quite well with the competition model of democracy, they are generally deficient in respect of these other conditions: there is not a rapid circulation of the personnel of the élites, which are still recruited predominantly from the upper class in society;[4] the outlook of the élites has changed only slowly, if at all, and the old aristocratic view of their functions is kept alive by their recruitment from the upper class, by the élite theories themselves, and by the prevailing social doctrines of 'getting on' and reaching 'the top'; and lastly, the 'levelling' of conditions in Western societies has proceeded so slowly and to such a limited extent that the rulers are still very sharply distinguished, economically and socially, from the ruled. It should be noted, too, that the political parties which stand at the centre of the competition between élites have themselves lost something of their democratic character with their transformation into mass parties. They may not have become, in most cases, quite the oligarchic organizations which Michels (1911) foresaw, but they are more easily dominated by their officials, and it is correspondingly more difficult for the rank and file members to have an effective influence in the shaping of policy.

Besides these political factors, we should also consider whether there are not more general social conditions which are essential to the life and growth of a democratic system of government. It is a notable feature of the recent élite theories that, having defined democracy as simply a *form of government of a whole society*, and thus excluded from the definition such important features as are embodied, for example, in the notions of 'social democracy', or 'industrial democracy', they go on to eliminate so far as possible even a consideration of the influence which this kind of extension of democracy may have upon the form of government itself. But this is to overlook or reject a fundamental idea of sociology – namely, that the institutions which exist in the different spheres of society are not merely co-existent but are connected with each other by relations of concordance or contradiction and mutually affect each other – which was admirably formulated by Marx (1844), in his criticism of the political philosophers of his day, when he argued that it was a profound error to separate the human being as a citizen (i.e. as an individual with political rights) completely from the human being as a member of civil society (i.e. as an individual engaged in family life and in economic production). Are we to suppose, for instance, that the modern Western family, in which the relations between the members are, generally speaking, more cooperative and less authoritarian than was the case in the nineteenth century, has come into being unaffected by democratic ideas of government; or that once it exists it has no significance for the maintenance and extension of democratic attitudes and practices in the sphere of government? Can we accept that democratic government, which requires of the individual independent judgement and active participation in deciding important social issues, will flourish when in one of the most important spheres of life – that of work and economic production – the great majority of individuals are denied the opportunity to take an effective part in reaching the decisions which vitally affect their lives? It does not seem to me that a person can live in a condition of complete and unalterable subordination for much of the time, and yet acquire the habits of responsible choice and self-government which political democracy calls for. It is true that in the Western societies the subordination of the individual at work is less onerous than it used to be in some respects; workers have some influence upon working conditions through the trade unions and through institutions of joint consultation and 'social partnership' which have developed in a rudimentary fashion, while the substantial increase in leisure time has enlarged the sphere in which they are able to decide things for themselves. On the other hand, much industrial work has become more subdivided and repetitive in modern times, with the result that workers, even if they are not subjected to the old type of authoritarian control by employers, still find less and less opportunity to exercise judgement, imagination, or skill in the performance of their tasks.[5]

There are other circumstances, more frequently discussed, which affect the practice of democratic government. Great inequalities of wealth and income plainly influence the extent to which individuals can participate in the activities of ruling the community. A rich man may have difficulty in entering the kingdom of heaven, but he will find it relatively easy to get into the higher councils of a political party, or into some branch of government. He can also exert an influence on political life in other ways: by controlling media of communication, by making acquaintances in the higher circles of politics, by taking a prominent part in the activities of pressure groups and advisory bodies of one kind or another. A poor man has none of these advantages: he has no relationships with influential people, he has little time or energy to devote to political activity, and little opportunity to acquire a thorough knowledge of political ideas or facts. It is equally evident that other categories of citizens – and notably women and members of particular ethnic groups – are, in a similar way though to a great extent for other reasons, grossly under-represented in the political élite, and this situation too has only recently begun to change, very gradually.

The differences which originate in economic and other inequalities are enhanced by educational differences. In most of the Western democracies the kind of education provided for those groups which mainly provide the rulers of the community is sharply differentiated from that which is provided for the much greater number of those who are ruled. Furthermore the educational system in most Western societies does not only consolidate the distinction between rulers and ruled; it keeps alive and flourishing the whole ideology of élite rule insofar as it emphasizes the selection of exceptional individuals for élite positions, and the rewards in income or status that scholastic achievement brings, rather than the raising of the general level of education throughout the community and the contribution which this might make to increasing the participation of the mass of citizens in government. The disparities of wealth and education which I have mentioned are aspects of the division of society into classes; and it is this fundamental division – to which other inequalities can be partially related – that has often been regarded, in the theories of 'social democracy' for example, as incompatible with democratic government. I shall discuss it further in the following chapter.

The objections which I have so far brought against the élite theories of democracy are based upon an alternative conception of democracy as 'government by the people'; but there are other objections which arise from inconsistencies within the élite theories themselves. First, there is the question as to whether any form of government could survive for long if there were permanent opposition and conflict between élites, and an incessant circulation of their personnel. Mannheim (1956), writing on the problems of political democracy in terms of the German situation of the early 1930s, argued that the growth of democracy means a loss of homogeneity in the governing élite, and went on to say: 'Modern democracy often breaks down because it is burdened with far more complex decision problems than those facing early democratic (or pre-democratic) societies with their more homogeneous ruling groups' (p. 172). T.S. Eliot (1948) argued in a similar fashion that élites, which require a regular circulation of their personnel, are unable to ensure social continuity in the way that the ruling classes of earlier times could do.[6] However, both writers exaggerated the dangers arising from these sources, for there has not been the substantial circulation of individuals between the élites and the rest of the population which they assumed, and the élites are not for the most part engaged in fundamental conflict with each other. As Aron (1950, p. 147) commented, in discussing the postwar situation of the Western societies:

> The composition of the governing élite may be progressively altered, the relative importance of the various groups in the élite may be changed, but a society can only survive and prosper if there is true collaboration between those groups. In one way or another there must be unity of opinion and action on essential points in the élite.

In fact, this unity of opinion and action – and the social continuity which Eliot desired – has been largely assured in the Western societies by the recruitment of élites from the upper class of society, and by the ideological support of the theory of élites itself. It is still broadly true that 'From the hour of their birth some are marked out for subjection and some for command' (Aristotle, *Politics*). In the Western societies the élites stand, for the most part, on one side of the great barrier constituted by class divisions; and so an entirely misleading view of political life is created if we concentrate our attention upon the competition between élites, and fail to examine the conflicts between classes and the ways in which élites are connected with the various social classes.

It is one of the political myths of our age that democracy is protected and sustained principally or solely by a competition between élites, which balance and limit each other's power. When we look at the arguments of the élite theorists in favour of this thesis we find a second inconsistency, which consists in moving, at different stages of the argument, from the concept of a plurality of élites to the quite different concept of a multiplicity of voluntary associations. Mosca, for example, referred to the possibility, in a democratic system, for many different 'social forces' (not élites) to take part in political life and to limit the power of other social forces, and especially bureaucracy. Similarly Aron (1950), when he urged the importance of the diffusion of power in the pluralistic democracies, did not invoke only the principal élites which he distinguished, but spoke of the great variety of professional and political organizations to be found in such societies, which set bounds to the power of the rulers. But this advocacy of flourishing voluntary associations as a vital condition for effective democracy does not lend support to the élite theories. For what is being asserted, when the importance of vigorous local government, professional associations and other voluntary and autonomous bodies is given such prominence, is not that those organizations are élites which are engaged in major struggles for political power, but that they provide so many occasions and opportunities for ordinary men and women to learn and practise the business of self-government. They are means through which government by the people is made more real and practical in a large, complex society.

Thus we are led by this path also to the view expressed earlier, that the preservation, and especially the development and improvement, of a democratic system of government does not depend primarily upon fostering the competition between small élite groups whose activities are carried on in realms far removed from the observation or control of ordinary citizens, but upon creating and establishing the conditions in which a large majority of citizens, if not all citizens, can and do take part in deciding those social issues which vitally affect their individual lives – at work, in the local community, and in the nation – and in which the distinction between élites and masses is reduced to the smallest possible degree. Such a view implies, first, that opportunities to extend the scope of self- government should be assiduously sought, especially in the sphere of economic production, where some postwar experiments such as the Yugoslav self-management system, community development projects in India and many other countries, and cooperative enterprises sponsored by public authorities, for all the difficulties they have encountered, deserve serious attention; and secondly, that the present hindrances to full participation in the government of voluntary associations and quasi-governmental bodies, which arise in the main from differences of social class, and are apparent in the predominance of upper-class and middle-class individuals as officials of such organizations, should in some way be overcome.

NOTES

1 The theory of games was used most extensively, however, in the study of international conflicts, notably in the once fashionable 'war-games'. Its uses in this field were critically examined by Aron (1966), in a concluding note on 'rational strategy' and 'reasonable politics' (pp. 751–70).

2 Aron (1950) says that 'it is quite impossible for the government of a society to be in the hands of any but a few . . . there is government *for* the people; there is no government *by* the people'.

3 Although he went on, somewhat inconsistently, to discuss the growth of equality and the reduction in the distance between élites and masses as factors in the development of modern democracy.

4 See above, Chapter 3, and also Guttsman (1963, chap. 11), where it is shown how few individuals are enabled to take part in the formulation of national policies. In Britain there is a small group of 'the good and the great' – at most a few thousand people, drawn predominantly from the upper class in society – who participate in the work of advisory committees, Royal Commissions and similar public bodies.

5 See, on these questions, Georges Friedmann (1956).

6 Eliot criticized the view that élites in modern societies can perform adequately the functions of earlier ruling classes without noticing that Mannheim himself had already formulated the criticism. In fact, Mannheim seems never to have reached a settled view of the place of élites in modern society. Sometimes he argued in favour of the competition between élites as a safeguard of democracy; at other times, he advocated rule by a single élite composed of the intellectuals; and finally he suggested that no élite, or group of élites, can ensure political stability unless it takes on the characteristics of a ruling class, possibly by association with an existing upper class, and becomes a hereditary and property-owning group. The only conception which Mannheim consistently excluded is that of a classless, egalitarian society.

Chapter 7

Equality or élites?

Democracy, in one of its established meanings, implies that there should be a substantial degree of equality among human beings, both in the sense that all the adult members of a society ought to have, so far as is possible, an equal influence upon those decisions which affect important aspects of the life of the society, and in the sense that inequalities of wealth, of social rank, or of education and access to knowledge, should not be so considerable as to result in the permanent subordination of some individuals and groups to others in any of the various spheres of social life, or to create great inequalities in the actual exercise of political rights. The advocates of equality have never been concerned to claim anything so foolish as that individuals are exactly alike or equal in physique, intelligence, or character. They have based their case upon a variety of other considerations, among which there are three which have a particular importance. The first is that for all their individual idiosyncrasies, human beings are remarkably alike in some fundamental respects: they have similar physical, emotional and intellectual needs. That is why there can be a science of nutrition, and in a less exact way, sciences of mental health and healing, and of the education of children. Furthermore, the range of variation in the qualities of individuals is relatively narrow, and there is a clustering about the middle of the range. If this were not so – if there were truly differences of kind, rather than of degree; if there were brute beasts at one extreme and angels or god-like beings at the other – then one of the factual supports of the egalitarian case would be removed.

The second point is that the individual differences among human beings and the social distinctions between them are two separate things.

Long ago, Rousseau (1755, p. 160) made this important distinction:

> I conceive that there are two kinds of inequality among the human species; one, which I call natural or physical, because it is established by nature, and consists in a difference of age, health, bodily strength, and the qualities of the mind or of the soul: and another, which may be called moral or political inequality, because it depends upon a kind of convention, and is established, or at least authorized, by the consent of men. This latter consists of the different privileges, which some men enjoy to the prejudice of others; such as that of being more rich, more honoured, more powerful or even in a position to exact obedience.

We cannot tell with any certainty how far these two kinds of inequality have been in correspondence in most of the societies which have existed up to modern times. The theory of the circulation of élites was intended in part to suggest that they were; that the most able individuals in every society succeeded in entering the élite, or in forming a new élite which in due course became pre-eminent. But we have seen earlier that the historical evidence produced in support of this thesis is quite inconclusive, and that the more abundant evidence available in the case of modern societies (which are generally regarded as displaying an exceptional degree of social mobility) does not confirm it. The major inequalities in society are in the main social products, created and maintained by the institutions of property and inheritance, of political and military power, and supported by particular beliefs and doctrines, even though they are never entirely resistant to the desire of ambitious individuals to climb the social ladder.

These considerations lead on to the third point which I have to make about the character of the egalitarian arguments. If neither inequality nor equality is a natural phenomenon, which has simply to be accepted, the advocacy of one or the other does not consist in the presentation of a scientific argument based wholly upon matters of fact, but in the formulation of a moral and social ideal. We can *opt* for equality, and although in so doing we have to pay attention to matters of fact which bear upon the practicability of the ideal and upon the means appropriate for attaining it, the ultimate justification for our option is not itself any matter of fact but a reasoned claim that the pursuit of equality is likely to create a more admirable society. In using the term 'we' I mean to refer particularly to people living in the societies of the twentieth century; for it was difficult in any earlier age to form a practical conception of a stable and durable egalitarian form of society, given the insecurity of economic life, the absence of effective means of communication, the inadequacy of education, and the lack of knowledge about social structure and individual character. The twentieth century is unique in offering for the first time the opportunity and the means to fashion social life according to human desires; and it is both hopeful and terrible for that reason.

It is not my purpose here to set out the moral case for equality,[1] but rather to consider the social and political problems which beset the pursuit of equality, and the criticisms, other than moral objections, which the élite theories bring against it. It will be convenient to begin by examining Marx's conception of a 'classless society', both because it presents the ideal of equality in a form which became more widely accepted than any other in the modern world, and because it was the principal source from which, by opposition, the élite theories themselves arose. Everyone knows that Marx did not write a blueprint for the socialist society which he envisaged and desired;[2] nevertheless, it is unmistakably clear from those of his writings which refer to the future socialist society what he regarded, in broad outline, as its distinctive features. Marx's sketch of this classless society incorporates moral, sociological and historical elements. The moral aspect is treated most fully in some of his early manuscripts, and particularly in the *Economic and Philosophical Manuscripts* of 1844, but it is by no means neglected in his later writings.[3] From this aspect a classless society is defined as one in which individuals would exercise a much greater, and more equal, control over their destinies; would be liberated from the tyranny of their own creations such as the state and bureaucracy, capital and technology; would be productive rather than acquisitive; would find pleasure and support in their social cooperation with others rather than antagonism and bitterness in the competition with them. Marx did not always express himself with the same optimism about the possibility of attaining this condition of society,[4] but he never ceased to regard it as the ideal. His notion of what would constitute self-determination for the individual was expressed in a variety of ways. In the first place, the individual had to be freed from determination by his class or occupation; as Marx wrote in *German Ideology* (1845–6):

the communal relationship into which the individuals of a class entered, and which was determined by their common interests over against a third party, was always a community to which these individuals belonged only as average individuals, only in so far as they lived within the conditions of existence of their class. It was a relationship in which they participated not as individuals but as members of a class. But with the community of revolutionary proletarians, who establish their control over the conditions of existence of themselves and the other members of society, it is just the reverse; the individuals participate as individuals. It is just this combination of individuals (assuming, of course, the advanced level of modern productive forces) which brings the conditions for the free development and activity of individuals under their own control; conditions which were formerly abandoned to chance and which had acquired an independent existence over against the separate individuals.

Secondly, the individual had to be freed from domination by a remote, inaccessible and unaccountable government and administration, and to participate as fully as possible in deciding issues of general social importance. Marx held up as a practical instance of such participation the Paris Commune, in which the functions of government were undertaken by municipal councillors, chosen by universal suffrage, responsible and revocable at short term, and in which all public functions from those of the members of the Commune downwards were performed at workmen's wages.

The sociological element in Marx's conception is to be found in his assertion that the principle of inequality is embodied in the institutions of social class – the division between owners of the means of production and non-owners – and more fundamentally in the division of labour in society, especially the division between manual and intellectual work. It follows that equality is to be attained by the abolition of classes, which will entail the suppression of the division of labour. Marx always insisted strongly upon this last condition. In *German Ideology* he expressed it in a somewhat romantic form:

as soon as the division of labour begins, each man has a particular, exclusive sphere of activity, which is forced upon him and from which he cannot escape. He is a hunter, a fisherman, a shepherd, or a critical critic, and must remain so if he does not want to lose his means of livelihood; whereas in communist society, where nobody has one exclusive sphere of activity but each can become accomplished in any branch he wishes, production as a whole is regulated by society, thus making it possible for me to do one thing today and another tomorrow, to hunt in the morning, fish in the afternoon, rear cattle in the evening, criticize after dinner, in accordance with my inclination, without ever becoming hunter, fisherman, shepherd or critic.

Later, however, in the first volume of *Capital* (1867), he conveyed the same idea in more realistic terms:

the detail-worker of today, the limited individual, the mere bearer of a particular social function, will be replaced by the fully developed individual, for whom the different social functions he performs are but so many alternative modes of activity. One step already spontaneously taken towards effecting this revolution is the establishment of technical and agricultural schools, and of *écoles d'enseignement professionel*, in which the children of the workingmen receive some instruction in technology and in the practical handling of the various implements of labour . . . There can be no doubt that when the working class comes into power . . . technical instruction, both theoretical and practical, will take its proper place in the working class schools.

Marx's argument, therefore, is directed just as much against the idea of functional élites – even élites recruited solely on the basis of merit – as against the idea of classes. The division of labour, and above all the division between those who think and plan and those who merely perform the necessary routine labour, continually recreates the class system; and it confines individuals within a sphere of life which they have not chosen for themselves and in which they cannot acquire the means to develop all their faculties.

The historical element in this conception has two aspects. First, Marx presents a historical scheme, applicable mainly within the area of Western civilization, in which the forms of domination and servitude – master and slave, feudal lord and serf, industrial capitalist and worker – constitute a series which is distinguished by an increasing awareness of the contrast between a person's qualities as an individual and his or her qualities as a member of a social category:

> in the course of historical development . . . there emerges a distinction between the personal life of the individual and his life as it is determined by some branch of labour and the conditions pertaining to it . . . In a system of estates (and still more in the tribe) this is still concealed: for instance, a nobleman is always a nobleman, a commoner always a commoner, irrespective of his other relationships, a quality inseparable from his individuality. The distinction between the personal and the class individual, the accidental nature of conditions of life for the individual, appears only with the emergence of class, which itself is a product of the bourgeoisie . . . The contradiction between the personality of the individual proletarian and the condition of life imposed on him, his labour, becomes evident to himself, for he is sacrificed from his youth onwards and has no opportunity of achieving within his own class the conditions which would place him in another class.
>
> (Marx and Engels 1845–6)

To this series Marx added a further term, the classless society of the future in which there would no longer be any sharp contrast between the personal qualities of the individual and the conditions of his or her social life, in which all individuals would be able to develop their faculties to the fullest extent and would experience limitation only as natural beings who are obliged to produce their material means of existence and are mortal.

Secondly, Marx regards the classless society as a form of society which is only conceivable, and can only be achieved, at the historical moment when capitalism attains its fullest development, because the consummation of capitalism produces for the first time a subject class – the proletariat – which contains within itself no elements of further social differentiation. When the proletariat has been liberated by the expropriation of the capitalist owners of industry it will create new social institutions which will express its own homogeneity and solidarity and preclude the formation of new privileged groups in society.

Few modern advocates of equality would dissent from Marx's moral ideal of the classless society; but they would undoubtedly question some of the sociological and historical arguments with which he explained the manner of its advent and defined its characteristics. They would object still more to what used to be the 'orthodox' or 'official' Marxist interpretation (now happily defunct) of the classless society, which reduced the concept to little more than a technical expression describing a state of affairs in which there is no significant private ownership of means of production. One major objection to Marx's own account must be that it portrays the attainment of a classless society – of genuine equality and liberty – as a once-for-all affair: at one moment human beings are living in the egoistic, acquisitive, conflict-ridden world of capitalism; at the next, prehistory has come to an end and they are engaged in creating the new institutions of a classless society. This is not quite fair to Marx inasmuch as he allows for a period of transition between capitalism and socialism – described occasionally by that phrase of ill-omen 'the dictatorship of the proletariat' – and for stages of development towards the 'higher phase of communist society' (Marx 1875). But it is fair in the sense that Marx never for a moment considers the possibility that under certain circumstances new social distinctions and a new ruling class might emerge in the society which succeeds capitalism; for example, from the dictatorship of the proletariat itself, which is so easily transformed into the tyranny of a party. This is a point of weakness in the Marxist doctrine which the élite theorists, and notably Michels (1911), attacked so successfully; and a new cogency was given to their criticisms by the bitter experience of the USSR and the East European countries under Stalin's rule. Thus, Aron (1950) described the classless society in the following terms:

There is still, however, in such a society, a small number of men who in practice run the industrial undertakings, command the army, decide what proportion of the national resources should be allocated to saving and investment and fix scales of remuneration. This minority has infinitely more power than the political rulers in a democratic society, because both political and economic power are concentrated in their hands ... Politicians, trade union leaders, public officials, generals and managers all belong to one party and are part of an authoritarian organization. The unified élite has absolute and unbounded power. All intermediate bodies, all individual groupings, and particularly professional groups, are in fact controlled by delegates of the élite, or, if you prefer it, representatives of the State ... A classless society leaves the mass of the population without any possible means of defence against the élite.

Aron then considers an objection to this account, namely that the idea of a classless society is being confused with a more or less accurate picture of Soviet society, and he admits that

a different type of classless society is in theory possible. In present conditions, however, other types of classless society are extremely unlikely. In order to avoid a monopoly of power in the hands of the group of men in control of the state, it would be necessary to restore a large number of centres of power; the various undertakings or trusts should become the property of those working in them, of local or trade union communities, instead of the centralized state. At the present time such decentralization is unlikely to come about, for psychological and technical reasons ... It is possible to conceive also that the élite in power might not constitute a sort of religious and military sect and might be organized as a democratic party. There again, however, the idea which is possible in theory is extremely unlikely in practice ... Even more, the ideological monopoly preserved by the élite in power seems to me to correspond to an inherent requirement in such a regime ... In short, the unification of the élite is inseparable from the concentration of all economic and political power in its hands and that concentration is itself inseparable from the planning of an entirely collectivized economy.

(ibid., pp. 131–2)

Is it possible to meet these objections and to formulate in a more acceptable way the ideal of an egalitarian society? Let us note, first, some important resemblances between the classless society in the USSR as it was described by Aron, and the mass society which Mills (1956, p. 304) portrayed as developing in the USA. In a mass society, which Mills contrasts with a democratic 'society of publics':

(1) far fewer people express opinions than receive them; for the community of publics becomes an abstract collection of individuals who receive impressions from the mass media. (2) The

communications that prevail are so organized that it is difficult or impossible for the individual to answer back immediately or with any effect. (3) The realization of opinion in action is controlled by authorities who organize and control the channels of such action. (4) The mass has no autonomy from institutions; on the contrary, agents of authorized institutions penetrate this mass, reducing any autonomy it may have in the formation of opinion by discussion.

Among the most important structural characteristics of both the classless society and the mass society are the decline or disappearance of intermediate organizations – voluntary associations small enough for the individual to have an effective say in their activities – and the increasing distance between the leaders and the masses in all types of organization. It is obvious that these characteristics are very much more pronounced in the Soviet-type societies than in the Western countries, where there is no political or legal bar to the formation of associations, and where open as well as hidden competition for the allegiance of the citizens takes place between the large organizations; but there are also some common features which have been produced by more general causes, among them the growth in size and power of organizations, and notably the multinational corporations, made possible by technological advances (in production, communication, etc.), the increasing influence and control exercised by the state over economic production, irrespective of the type of economy, which was determined very largely by the massive production of war materials, and the international rivalry between nations organized on a semi-war footing, which is favourable to the growth of centralized and authoritarian political leadership.

Not all of these adverse influences can be combated effectively within the limits of a single society; they also call for changes in the relations between nations. Those problems which can be dealt with on a national level arise very largely from the size and complexity of organizations and from the authoritarian tendencies implicit in highly centralized economic planning. The attempt to solve them has to proceed along several different lines, some of which have been indicated in the previous chapter – the greatest possible decentralization of political authority by the transfer of responsibility for decisions, wherever feasible, to local and regional councils and to voluntary associations, and the extension of self-government to the economic field by the creation of appropriate new institutions, such as a system of self-management. The danger that a new ruling class of political bosses and industrial managers will be formed in a socialized economy can be met, not only by the introduction of self-government in the enterprise, but also by limiting the scope of collective ownership. It does not seem to me at all necessary to the attainment of an egalitarian society that all small- and medium-scale manufacturing, semi-artisan production, agriculture, retail trading and the provision of services of diverse kinds should be absorbed into large publicly owned enterprises and agencies. At the least, this should be treated as a practical question, and any propensity of such private economic activities to engender new social classes and new systematic inequalities should be analysed in the light of experience. Similarly, the dangers of an intellectual dictatorship can be met by giving a large degree of autonomy to educational and cultural organizations.

In the intellectual sphere it is particularly important that there should be independent associations which compete with each other; not only in the case of sound and television broadcasting and the press, but also in book publishing and in scientific research. But this requirement is quite compatible with some degree of public ownership. The associations could well be owned or effectively controlled by their members, while being supported to a large extent by public funds and subject to general regulation by a national authority. This is already the situation of universities in most Western countries, although there has been a marked tendency since the early 1980s to subject them to greater government regulation, especially in Britain. The same principle can be applied also to the operation of industry and commerce. The individual enterprises may be owned and most of their policies decided upon by those who work in them, and they may compete with each other in respect of price and quality at least as effectively as privately owned enterprises do – or are supposed to do – while being subject to controls of various kinds in the interests of a national economic plan. The achievements of a system of this kind, which combines public ownership with a form of market economy, such as existed in Yugoslavia until the 1980s, show that although there are many practical difficulties this is a viable form of economic organization and no longer simply a Utopian dream. There does not seem to be any reason for supposing that in advanced industrial societies, which do not have to engage in the arduous business of primary capital accumulation, the control of the economy as a whole by a central planning authority need be any more rigorous or authoritarian under a system of public ownership such as that which I have outlined than under a private enterprise system; for in both cases there will be very similar problems to be faced and similar techniques can be employed. In France, for example, the postwar economic planners had very considerable powers and they were not subject to any close control by the elected representatives of the people.

These considerations are sufficient, I think, to cast serious doubt upon Aron's assertion that it would be impossible to achieve, in a socialized economy, a genuine decentralization of power, or to escape intellectual and cultural uniformity. It is true, of course, that even in a classless society which had carried decentralization very far, and in which numerous independent associations flourished, there would have to exist some fundamental agreement among the members of society upon the general features of its organization. But this must be the case in any society which is to endure, and as we have seen, those who regard democracy as being sustained by a plurality of competing élites still introduce the qualification that the competition must not be pushed to extremes and that there must be an underlying consensus of opinion. The hope of those who advocate equality is that the experience of living in a society which was drawing rapidly closer to this ideal would gradually persuade individuals of its value. If this occurred, there would still remain all manner of intellectual disagreements and of choices as to a personal way of life, but there would be general agreement upon the desirability of social equality and opposition to those inequalities which produce and maintain lasting distinctions between whole categories of people.

Let me now return to another problem which is posed by Marx's conception of a classless society. According to Marx, the division of labour is not only in itself an impediment to the full development of each individual, a form of bondage, but is also the source from which arise the major social classes, which establish still more obdurate limitations of human freedom. The division of labour has, therefore, to be 'overcome': that is, abolished and transcended. But does it make sense to speak of 'abolishing' the division of labour in a modern industrial society? At first sight the problem seems more intractable now than in Marx's own day, for the specialization of occupations, including intellectual occupations, has proceeded rapidly, and in the sphere of industrial mass production the subdivision of tasks has reached a point where the individual worker appears more and more as an adjunct to the machine, whose daily work is confined to the performance of a few simple, thoughtless and repetitive movements. Nevertheless, there have been other changes in work, and a new range of possibilities can now be seen, which make Marx's vision of the future a great deal more plausible. First, there have been changes in the nature of occupations, brought about especially by the development of automation. The effect of automation is to eliminate large numbers of workers on the assembly line and to replace them by more educated and responsible individuals whose function is to supervise very complicated chains of production which are controlled in detail by machines. At present these changes affect only a small part of industry, but they will become increasingly important. Secondly, the high productivity of modern industry has already made possible a reduction of working hours, and its accelerating rate of growth will bring within the capacity of all the advanced industrial countries, in the next decade or two, the establishment of a working week of some twenty-five or thirty hours. These countries are about to produce a new and revolutionary pheno-menon: namely, a 'leisure class' which comprises the whole population.[5] Thirdly, if there were introduced in publicly owned industries the kind of self-management which I discussed earlier, and if this type of public ownership were established in all large enterprises, the range of the work activities of manual and clerical workers could be considerably extended. The individual worker would no longer be confined within a specialized task, but would also take part in the planning and management of production.

Together, these various changes in the organization of working life would modify profoundly the meaning of the division of labour. Individuals with abundant leisure would have the opportunity, as Marx believed, to engage in more than one activity, to express themselves in diverse fields of endeavour, both physical and intellectual; and even as economic producers they would find more occasion to develop all-round abilities by participating in the work of management and by learning something of the science and technology upon which the operations of industry are based. The division of labour would become more evidently a technique which human beings need to use in producing their means of life, but which they must also control; it would no longer shape and constrict the whole of their lives, turning one person irrevocably into a worker on the assembly line, another into a clerk, and a third into a tycoon. Such changes imply, and they are already beginning to produce, a great expansion of education in all its forms – an extension of the period of universal secondary education, higher education for a large proportion of those between the ages of 18 and 21, adult education on a growing scale, with special facilities for those who decide at a mature age to prepare themselves for a new occupation – and more lavish public provision of facilities for sport and recreation. Perhaps I may conclude this discussion, and at the same time illustrate how slowly new and radical ideas make their way in the world, by quoting from one of the most eminent of British economists, whose vision of the role of labour in a future society seems quite close to that of Marx. Alfred Marshall, in an essay on 'The future of the working classes' (1873, pp. 101–18), wrote:

That men do habitually sustain hard corporeal work for eight, ten or twelve hours a day, is a fact so familiar to us that we scarcely realize the extent to which it governs the moral and mental history of the world; we scarcely realize how subtle, all-pervading and powerful may be the effect of the work of man's body in dwarfing the growth of the man . . . Work, in its best sense, the healthy energetic exercise of faculties, is the aim of life, is life itself; and in this sense every one [in the ideal society which Marshall conceives] would be a worker more completely than now. But men would have ceased to carry on mere physical work to such an extent as to dull their higher energies. In the bad sense, in which work crushes a man's life, it would be regarded as wrong. The active vigour of the people would continually increase; and in each successive generation it would be more completely true that every man was by occupation a gentleman . . . that condition which we have pictured . . . a condition in which every man's energies and abilities will be fully developed – a condition in which men will work not less than they do now but more; only, to use a good old phrase, most of their work will be a work of love; it will be a work which, whether conducted for payment or not, will exercise and nurture their faculties. Manual work, carried to such an excess that it leaves little opportunity for the free growth of his higher nature, that alone will be absent. In so far as the working classes are men who have such excessive work to do, in so far will the working classes have been abolished.

So far I have considered mainly those objections to the idea of a classless, egalitarian society which take as their principal theme the dangers of intellectual tyranny and political dictatorship. There is, however, another important line of criticism which brings to light a different aspect of the problem of élites. It has often been maintained, in one form or another, that the advancement of civilization has depended, and does always depend, upon the activities of small minorities of exceptionally gifted people. Ortega y Gasset (1930, p. 49) made such a claim:

> As one advances in life, one realizes more and more that the majority of men – and of women – are incapable of any other effort than that strictly imposed on them as a reaction to external compulsion. And for that reason, the few individuals we have come across who are capable of a spontaneous and joyous effort stand out isolated, monu-mentalized, so to speak, in our experience. These are the select men, the nobles, the only ones who are active and not merely reactive, for whom life is a perpetual striving, an incessant course of training.

In a similar manner, Clive Bell (1928) argued that a civilized society is characterized by reasonableness and a sense of values, and that these qualities can be produced, implanted and sustained only by an élite. Now some part of what is asserted by these writers is undoubtedly true: namely, that civilization has sometimes been greatly advanced by the work of exceptional individuals – though it has also been greatly retarded on many occasions by the activities of other notable 'leaders and teachers' of humanity. But this is not to say that people of the former kind, with their associates or followers, form a social élite, still less that they are in the majority of cases a ruling élite. They may have little social prestige, or be treated with active disdain by the rulers of society; they may be dependent financially upon the patronage of an upper class, without forming part of it. Their contribution to society is of an individual kind, not ordinarily dependent upon the formation of a distinctive social group;

very often it is more strongly affected by the support and enthusiasm which their work calls forth in a whole population (as in fifth-century Athens) or in a whole class (as in Renaissance Italy or in eighteenth-century France). Exceptional individuals might perhaps be regarded as forming an élite in the first of the senses which Pareto gave to the term – namely, the category of those who have the highest ability in their branch of activity – except that in this sense many activities which have little or nothing to do with the advance of civilization would be included, and that the élites so defined would be made up of talented individuals rather than of those who have exceptional creative powers. It would really be better to use some other term; for example, the term 'creative minority', which Arnold Toynbee (1934–61, vol. 3, p. 239) seemed to be using to refer, not to an élite group, but to a simple plurality of individuals, when he observed that: 'In all acts of social creation the creators are either creative individuals or, at most, creative minorities.'[6]

Those who attempt to defend the élite doctrines by referring to the importance of intellectual and artistic creativity commit two errors: first, they neglect the vital interplay between creative individuals and the society in which they live – which is perhaps most evident in the case of scientific work, but is also to be traced in the history of painting or architecture, in literature, in religious movements and in moral reforms – and secondly, they assume that such individuals associate together as an élite or élites which can exist only in a hierarchically ordered society, and which can exist best in a society divided into stable and enduring classes. In this last conception, as it is expressed, for example, by T.S. Eliot (1948), the subject of discussion is apt to change from the creation of culture to the transmission of culture. In Eliot's view there are, in every complex society, a number of levels of culture; it is important for the health of society that these different levels should be related to each other, but also that they should remain distinct, and that the manners and taste of society as a whole should be influenced by the highest culture. This can happen only, since culture is transmitted primarily through the family, if there exists an upper class composed of families which are able to maintain over several generations a settled way of life. Eliot admits that the existence of an upper class does not guarantee a high culture: 'the "conditions of culture" which I set forth do not necessarily produce the higher civilization: I assert only that when they are absent, the higher civilization is unlikely to be found' (p. 49). Nevertheless, it *may* be found. We have as yet no direct experience of the way of life of an egalitarian society, and we can do no more than estimate the probability of its being able to create and preserve a high level of culture. Creation is an individual act, but it is facilitated by a general enthusiasm and liveliness in society at large, and we may reasonably expect that an egalitarian society, in which leisure was widespread and individuals were encouraged to develop their talents, would be at least as creative as those which accomplished great things in earlier periods when the economic conditions and the class structure of society were being rapidly transformed.

As to the conservation and transmission of a high culture, we may well dissent from the view that it has been, and must be, primarily the work of the family. In the past, many other social groups – religious associations, philosophical schools, academies – have been at least as important as the family in transmitting culture; the family, i.e. the families of the upper class in society, have usually passed on, if they have passed on at all, something that has been conserved and kept alive elsewhere, by associations which enjoyed no great stability of membership from generation to generation. In a classless society the distance between high culture and lower types of culture would be less great, while regional and local diversity might become more pronounced; and the cultural heritage would be handed on, even more than in the past, by educational institutions and voluntary associations of every kind, and less than formerly by particular families. It is possible, too, that the conservation of culture, which is bound up inextricably in present-day societies with the maintenance of class privileges, would be less strongly emphasized – or at least change its aspect – and come to be taken much more for granted; while the power to create new forms of culture, to make new discoveries in the arts and sciences, would be more highly regarded and encouraged.

The theorists of élites defend, by these various means, the legacy from the inegalitarian societies of the past, while making concessions to the spirit of equality. They insist strongly upon an absolute distinction between rulers and ruled, which they present as a scientific law, but they reconcile democracy with this state of affairs by defining it as competition between élites. They accept and justify the division of society into classes, but endeavour to make this division more palatable by describing the upper classes as élites, and by suggesting that the élites are composed of the most able individuals, regardless of their social origins. Their case depends, to a large extent, upon substituting for the idea of equality the idea of equality of opportunity. But this latter notion, besides having quite a different moral significance, is actually self-contradictory. Equality of opportunity, as the expression is habitually used, presupposes inequality, since 'opportunity' means 'the opportunity to rise to a higher level in a stratified society'. At the same time, it presupposes equality, for it implies that the inequalities embedded in this stratified society have to be counteracted in every generation so that individuals can really develop their personal abilities; and every investigation of the conditions for equality of opportunity, for example in the sphere of education, has shown how strong and pervasive is the influence upon individual life-chances of the entrenched distinctions of social class. Equality of opportunity would become a reality only in a society without classes or élites, and the notion itself would then be otiose, for the equal life-chances of individuals in each new generation would be matters of fact, and the idea of opportunity would signify, not the struggle to rise into a higher social class, but the possibility for each individual to develop fully those qualities of intellect and sensibility which he or she has as a person, in an unconstrained association with others.

NOTES

1 It is admirably expounded in R.H. Tawney's book *Equality* (1952).
2 Surprisingly, this is often held against him, instead of being regarded as a mark of wisdom, and of profound faith in the creative capacities of human beings which were manifest even within the constraints of class societies and would be so much more easily made effective when those constraints were removed.
3 See, for example, his discussion in *Capital*, vol. I (1867), of the means to overcome the harmful effects of the division of labour, and in *Capital*, vol. III (1894), of the conditions of human freedom; his praise of the Paris Commune for its institution of genuinely democratic self-government, in *The Civil War in France* (1871); and his comments upon the programme of the Socialist Workers' Party of Germany in *Critique of the Gotha Programme* (1875).
4 For instance, in the passage on human freedom in *Capital*, vol. III (1894), chap. 48, Marx declared that the sphere of economic production is a realm of

necessity 'under any possible mode of production'; and 'The realm of freedom only begins, in fact, where that labour which is determined by need and external purpose, ceases; it is therefore, by its very nature, outside the sphere of material production proper.'

5 The division of labour and the growth of leisure are examined at length from a point of view which is very similar to my own in Georges Friedmann (1956).

6 However, in his concluding volume, in which he reconsiders his work, Toynbee approaches more closely the élite theories in saying:

> By a creative minority I mean a ruling minority in which the creative faculty in human nature finds opportunities for expressing itself in effective action for the benefit of all participants in the society ... By a dominant minority I mean a ruling minority that rules less by attraction and more by force.

(vol. 12, p. 305).

Chapter 8

Into the millennium

Many of those who were active in the radical movements of the 1960s were inspired by millennial hopes and dreams, most fervently expressed in the 'Port Huron Statement' of Students for a Democratic Society (Jacobs and Landau 1966, pp. 149–62) with its emphasis on participatory democracy, creative work, a socially regulated economy and the development of non-violent relationships within and between nations. But the millennium we are actually about to enter has a much harsher complexion. The world economy is dominated by 500 of the largest multinational corporations, by the nation states in which they have their headquarters, and by those institutions of world capitalism such as the World Bank and the International Monetary Fund which determine and regulate economic development on a global scale. These economic forces, which have concentrated the wealth of the planet to an unprecedented degree, have also impoverished a large part of the Third World of 'developing countries' and caused massive damage to the natural environment. The advanced (or relatively advanced) industrial countries, with at most 25 per cent of the world's population, consume 80 per cent of its energy resources and receive 85 per cent of total world income, while in the poorer countries 2,000 million people live in abject poverty or starve. Within the rich nations themselves there are great inequalities between a wealthy upper class and its affiliated élites, and those who live in relative, and sometimes extreme, poverty (by the average standards of their society), whose numbers have been increasing steadily since the end of the 1970s as unemployment has grown in conditions of worsening economic depression.

The circumstances in which humanity approaches the new millennium have many different aspects. In a very broad context we should consider the possibility that the human race, as a result of the cumulative destruction of the natural environment, will not survive far beyond the end of the twenty-first century, or will survive only in more primitive social forms; and the probability that in the shorter term there will be increasingly violent conflict – between North and South, among old and new nation states, and within individual states – as the struggle for resources and economic growth intensifies and the disintegration of society proceeds. Here, however, I am primarily concerned – although the various issues are connected – with an analysis of the role of upper classes and élites in the process of economic and social development (and decay) over the past three decades and for the medium-term future. What is clear initially is that since the 1970s the dominance of these classes and élites has been consolidated and reinforced, as a result of several factors. First, the power and influence of multinational corporations has greatly increased. Secondly, a change of political mood in the industrial countries favoured, and was then in turn strengthened by, the emergence of doctrines of the 'New Right' which proclaimed the superiority of free-market economies with minimal government intervention, lauded the role of the business élite, asserted an extreme individualism, and accepted or even welcomed a gross commercialization of social life and the growth of inequality. These changes in the industrial countries were then transmitted to the developing countries, as I have indicated in Chapter 5 above, by the various international agencies of world capitalism, resulting in the creation of Third World élites largely committed to Western economic models and interests. Thirdly, the collapse of the Communist regimes in Eastern Europe at the end of the 1980s was presented in the mass media, which are now predominantly owned by capitalist interests, as vindicating the claims of the free-marketeers, and the latter were quick to purvey their nostrums to the confused and insecure new regimes. As a result the countries of Eastern Europe, having rid themselves of the Communist dictatorships, embarked on the re-establishment of a capitalist economy – in some cases in an extreme *laissez-faire* form – rather than undertaking the kind of democratic socialist reconstruction of society which was the alternative option. In Eastern Europe, consequently, new upper classes and élites similar to those in the advanced industrial countries are being formed, but in conditions of widespread impoverishment, chaos and conflict which resemble in some respects those of the Third World.

The present dominance of capitalism, and the revival of élitism, should not, however, be regarded as having been definitively and securely established. Far from it. The capitalist industrial countries themselves are experiencing a severe crisis, in which there are both short-term and longer-term conditioning factors. The short-term prospect is one of continuing economic depression, large-scale unemployment and increasing poverty for the bottom 20 or 25 per cent of the population, for which no remedy has been convincingly outlined or implemented, although there are plenty of bland assurances of imminent recovery by sundry élite personages. If we were to adopt a business cycle schema such as that of Schumpeter (1939), based on the Kondratiev 'long waves', we should have to say that the present conditions are those of the depressive phase of the cycle, and that the onset of a new expansionary phase depends upon new technological advances and the subsequent innovating activity of a swarm of entrepreneurs (who, according to Schumpeter's later views, may be individuals, but more probably will be either private or public corporations).[1] But there is little indication at present that new inventions on a par with railways, motor cars, or computers will provide the required impetus in the near future. Furthermore, the upturn in the economic cycle, and the general trend of economic growth, was strongly influenced in the past by factors external to the economy, and notably by population growth and war. The present growth of world population, however, is taking place mainly in Third World countries which are too poor and burdened with foreign debts to provide major markets for consumer or investment goods; while in the industrial countries populations are for the most part either stationary or beginning to decline. War and preparations for war also played an important part in past recoveries from depression, and notably in the 1930s, but the end of the 'cold war' and the general reduction of military expenditure in the industrial countries – even though they continue to supply the weapons for many local wars – means that this is not likely to be a significant 'expansionary' factor in the foreseeable future. Ironically, it seems that the 'collapse of Communism' may be followed by the 'collapse of capitalism'.

There are also some more general considerations to be taken into account. Insofar as capitalism requires continuous economic growth,[2] even though interrupted by periodic crises, its further development may now be more severely constrained by the limits to natural resources; and in recent years strong ecology movements and parties have entered political life, advocating economic policies which are essentially opposed to the spirit of capitalism. On the other side, the period of most rapid and sustained postwar economic growth, from 1950–73, which Maddison (1982, pp. 96–7) called the 'golden age', was characterized in Western Europe, and in differing degrees elsewhere, by greatly increased government intervention in the economy, some economic planning and a limited movement towards more equal economic and social conditions, particularly as a result of full employment and improved social services. Since the later 1970s this movement has been reversed in many countries, but the reversal itself now encounters growing criticism and opposition.

What effect, then, have the economic and social convulsions of the past three decades had upon the élite doctrines and the responses to them? From a recent study of Mosca's thought and the élitist theories (Albertoni 1987) two main themes emerge. One is the possibility of interpreting Mosca's ideas in a more liberal and democratic sense (Albertoni 1987, pp. 135–40), especially in the light of his later writings and his criticism of the Fascist regime in Italy. Thus, in a letter of 1934 replying to some comments by his friend Guglielmo Ferrero he expressed the view that the root of political wrongs lies in the greatest anomaly of the modern world – the contradiction between political equality and economic inequality[3] – which remains innocuous only in periods and countries of general prosperity; and at the end of his *Storia delle dottrine politiche* (1937) he advocated 'mixed regimes' in which

neither the autocratic nor the liberal system is totally predominant and there is a slow but continual renewal of the political class . . . What is needed is the multiplicity and balance of ruling forces that is found only in a very advanced society.

(Albertoni 1987, p. 101)

From this aspect Mosca's later views can be seen as proposing a reconciliation of élite rule with democracy, such as Schumpeter and Mannheim in different ways also attempted (see Chapter 6 above). But the full implications of the 'great anomaly' of political equality and economic inequality remain unexamined in his work, and the question of the relation between élites and classes remains unresolved. This constitutes, therefore, a second major theme of recent discussion.

One important contribution to the debate is the study by T. H. Marshall (1950) which, although it was not directly concerned with élites, nevertheless formulated the central issues with great clarity. Marshall conceived democracy as a growth of citizenship – a progressive extension of civil, political and social rights – and noted that democracy in this sense embodied a principle of equality which is in conflict with ('at war with') the capitalist class system (ibid., p. 18). This idea of citizenship has been enormously influential, particularly in the last decade, and I shall discuss some of its ramifications later. First, however, let us examine more closely the problem of the relation between élites and classes. Albertoni (1987) discusses several postwar 'neo-élitist' doctrines, giving particular attention to Schumpeter (ibid., pp. 160–1), but concludes that in spite of the efforts to integrate élite conceptions with liberal-democratic and pluralist currents of thought in Western societies, they have 'failed to link up actively and definitively with both the fixed values which have always existed and inspired political action, and with the various social and economic interests that form the no less important programmatic aspects of such values' (ibid., p. 163). He also observes that the changes in the élitist doctrines 'show the ideological and doctrinal effects of the widespread influence and popularity of socialism, in the broadest sense of the term . . . Welfare-statism . . . is a doctrine and practice particularly significant in this respect' (ibid., p. 161).

It is evident from most of the recent contributions that what is being discussed is the political élite – that is to say, Mosca's 'governing élite' or more broadly his 'political class' – and this clarifies two essential issues. First, the more general concept of élites has become redundant, or at any rate has fallen into disuse. In the modern industrial countries there are numerous important 'functional élites' – scientists, technologists, managers, administrators, teachers and so on, and also, insofar as these countries are creating a civilization rather than merely a commercialized mass consumption society, artists and intellectuals – but there is no particular reason for referring to them as 'élites' at all. They are simply functional (largely occupational) *groups* within the social division of labour, whose members differ greatly in ability and achievement. But secondly, the conception of a political élite – more broadly or narrowly defined – which is at the centre of neo-élitist analyses, raises a host of questions about élites, classes and democracy, various aspects of which I have discussed in the preceding chapters, and which I shall now examine further in the perspective of recent social changes.

The first issue to be considered here is whether there are any convincing examples in the twentieth century of a 'ruling élite' or 'power élite'. In earlier chapters I have argued, while noting some possible exceptions (see pp. 29–30 above), that domination in most historical forms of society has been exercised by a class – a warrior nobility, landowners, industrial capitalists – whose position as the rulers of society is based upon ownership or effective possession of the major productive resources; and not by élite groups which can be defined by other criteria. With respect to modern capitalist societies in particular I have outlined reasons for rejecting the claims that a new élite of bureaucrats or managers has been establishing itself in power; and also the similar claims concerning the role of bureaucrats or intellectuals in the new nations of the Third World.

Nevertheless, some problematic cases have emerged in recent times. One is that of the military regimes which were installed in some countries (chiefly, but not exclusively, in the Third World) at various times during the twentieth century. These regimes, however, were not all alike: some were reformist or revolutionary, others – especially since 1945 – counter-revolutionary, and this fact indicates that in addition to the specific circumstances which gave military officers an exceptionally prominent role in society major class allegiances were also involved (see pp. 81–3 above). A second case is that of societies in which a political party established itself in power, suppressed all rival political forces, and inaugurated what could be regarded as a system of élite rule by the party leadership and a network of lesser functionaries – the two outstanding examples being the Soviet Union and National Socialist Germany. But here too, although we have to pay serious attention to the new political phenomenon of the development of mass parties, an analysis of the conditions in which these parties gained and consolidated their power cannot proceed very far without examining the class structure and class relations. In both Germany and the Soviet Union the party (and its specialized apparatuses such as the secret police) constituted the principal basis of political domination, and in that sense we can speak of a unified 'power élite', regulating a totalitarian system. At the same time, however, this type of political system involved a substantial degree of control over the national economy, most obviously in the Soviet Union, where, it can be argued, a 'new class' emerged which had effective possession, if not legal ownership, of the principal means of production.[4] Thus, while the role of the military or of a mass party, in some countries and during certain periods, may create a distinctive type of power élite, this élite is still intimately connected with major social classes or may give rise to new class formations.

At all events it is evident that in the present-day world, dominated by the leading capitalist countries, classes and class relations have the most potent influence on the character of political rule. In consequence, élite theory has virtually ceased to be expounded as a comprehensive alternative to class theory, or to the various theories of 'new social movements'; and the principal discussions of élites and élitism now concern primarily their relation to democracy. This theme was already prominent in some earlier studies, but it was given a new salience by the radical movements of the 1960s and it has continued to occupy a large place in recent debates, especially with reference to citizenship and to the restoration (or in many cases the attempted creation for the first time) of democratic regimes in Eastern Europe.

These debates involve in the first place very different conceptions of democracy, which I considered in Chapter 6 above, but which can now be more extensively analysed in the light of changes that have taken place over the past three decades. A broad distinction can be drawn between what may be called 'liberal democracy' and 'participatory democracy', though there are also diverse formulations within each category.[5] The first conception expresses what I have characterized as a 'static' view, according to which democracy has been finally achieved, in varying forms to be sure, in the modern industrial societies and to some extent elsewhere, through universal suffrage and the creation of political systems in which several parties compete freely for the support of a mass electorate. The liberal view emphasizes *representative* government and largely rejects the idea that citizens can, in any significant sense, govern *themselves*; and as we have seen this leads in some modern theories to a conception of democracy as being no more than a competitive struggle between political élites for the votes of a largely passive electorate. Against this, however, the so-called 'liberal-pluralist' theories introduce another political factor, namely pressure groups, which are held to express more directly the interests of particular groups of citizens, and to constrain in some degree the actions of political parties and of the centralized state. One feature of this view is that it assigns a more active role to the electorate (or at any rate to some parts of it), though if a wide-ranging pluralism is to be identified and advocated it needs to be extended to take account of social movements, which may mobilize much larger numbers of people.

Social movements, however, unlike pressure groups, generally have broader aims which look to the state of society as a whole, and in many cases advocate fundamental changes in the economic and social structure, so that their purposes and actions are in fact more closely related to the second conception I have distinguished – 'participatory democracy'. Indeed, it was the social movements of the 1960s which imparted a new vitality to this idea. What is expressed in it, first of all, is the view that democracy is itself a 'movement' which is still very far from its ultimate goal of establishing a form of society in which 'government by the people' becomes a reality. The proponents of participatory democracy therefore advocate, and analyse the conditions for, a continuous process of extending democracy, both within and outside the political system, and notably in the economic sphere of labour and production.

Let us consider, first, the ways in which democracy might be extended in the political system itself. There are numerous projects and movements devoted to this end, and we may take as an instructive example Charter 88 in Britain which campaigns for a new constitutional settlement that would include a Bill of Rights to establish civil liberties; freedom of information and open government; an electoral system of proportional representation; replacement of the House of Lords by a democratic, non-hereditary second chamber; subordination of the political executive to parliament and of all state agencies to the rule of law; the independence of a reformed judiciary; legal remedies for abuses of power by the state and its officials; an equitable distribution of power between the nations composing the United Kingdom and between local, regional and central government; and a written constitution anchored in the idea of universal citizenship. Some of these goals have already been attained in other modern democracies, and Britain – with a system of government that remains semi-feudal and exceptionally élitist – is undoubtedly less democratic than a number of other developed countries. This is not to say, however, that participatory democracy cannot also be greatly extended elsewhere; and some of the major issues are illuminated by the development of supra-national organizations, especially in Western Europe.

The European Community, at the present time, is far from being a thoroughly democratic political system; not because decisions are taken by 'bureaucrats in Brussels', but because they are taken, behind closed doors, by a Council of Ministers which is appointed by member governments, while the elected European Parliament has only limited powers. Furthermore, the very size, complexity and remoteness of a supra-national political system makes democratic participation and control more difficult, and the vaguely defined notion of 'subsidiarity' which the EC has formulated seems at present to mean little more than accepting the right of member states not to implement some Community policies of which they disapprove. Thus the 'social chapter' in the project for a more integrated Community, which attempts in a modest way to extend democratic participation in economic and social decision-making, has been rejected by the British government. Effective participatory democracy, on the other hand, requires a much more radical devolution of power within nation states themselves, to regional and local authorities whose policies can be more closely observed and influenced by the public. It also requires an extension of democracy into the process of production, both of goods and services (including education, health care and social welfare), by the introduction of appropriate forms of self-management[6] and representation of consumers. The extent to which such goals can be attained or more closely approached, and by what means, is a large subject, outside the scope of the present book, and I intend to examine it in a separate study. What is clear at all events is that there are increasingly powerful movements in the advanced industrial countries which are campaigning in several directions for fundamental changes in the structure of power, not only in the formal institutions of government but in the social system as a whole.

There are, therefore, major currents of anti-élitist thought and doctrine in the industrial countries, and to some extent elsewhere, which find expression in various forms; as projects for the reform of political institutions, for the extension of democracy into new areas of social life, or for the growth of citizenship, particularly in the sphere of social rights. What is being asserted is a principle of equality, in opposition to a social system in which there is a massive concentration of power in the hands of small groups of people who may be described as 'élites', or more accurately as 'upper classes'. On the other side, however, there are strong élitist tendencies – emanating naturally enough from some élites themselves and especially those constituting the 'political class' – which manifest themselves in various forms: (i) the gradual transformation of party electoral campaigns into media circuses in which the role of the party leader is invested with as much glamour and 'charisma' as is attainable; (ii) the regular convocation of 'summit meetings' at which world leaders are supposed to confer seriously and effectively about solutions to global problems, but which are also largely media events; (iii) the tendency towards an increasing centralization of power in many political parties themselves, which enhances the role of some leader or leading group while restricting opportunities for the members at large to express alternative views or to initiate fundamental debates about policy; (iv) a resistance in some countries, and notably in Britain, to a reform of electoral systems which would make possible the effective representation in government of substantial minority groups; and (v) a general hostility to social movements which become active and influential outside the sphere of party politics.

These élitist counter-currents are, however, less effective than their authors would desire. In most of the developed democratic countries there is widespread disillusionment with, and cynicism or indifference about, the actions of political élites, manifested partly in large-scale abstention from voting (notably in the USA), but also in the continuing growth of new social movements whose aims range from the assertion of regional and local interests to direct action against environmental damage, and in the attempts by green movements in particular to discover a form of party organization which would be less hierarchical, bureaucratic and élitist. More generally it may be argued, as Albertoni does, that modern 'neo-élitism' – that is to say, élitism modified by welfare-state, liberal-democratic and socialist conceptions – although it has given rise to numerous empirical studies[7] and to reformulations of élite theory,[8] contains 'an unresolved question which is not simply theoretical but ideological'; namely, 'what are the moral values and practical ends which today inspire the new élites?' And he goes on to say that 'we are still waiting for an unambiguous political doctrine', based on neo-élitist analyses, that would be 'feasible within the context of the substantially participatory and mass form of democracy in contemporary society' (Albertoni 1987, pp. 162–3).

It may be questioned, though, whether the present capitalist democracies, even taking into account the activities of numerous social movements, are as 'participatory' as this comment suggests, and whether the main problem is in fact that of reformulating élite moral values and practical aims, rather than exploring ways in which the autonomous and self-governing actions of citizens might be further extended. This second alternative, as I have indicated, raises complex issues into which I cannot enter here, but what is quite clear is that in any large society or association government or management has to be representative,[9] and that a realistic conception of participatory democracy must undoubtedly incorporate some elements of the liberal theory, while attempting to go beyond it. One major question then concerns the 'representativeness' of management or government, which involves not only the kind of reforms in political institutions that I have briefly considered, but still more the extension of representation to the sphere of work and production. Such an extension of democracy, or in other terms of the content of citizenship, implies a generally anti-élitist rather than a neo-élitist view, with the main emphasis placed on human equality, as I have argued in the previous chapter.

The end of the twentieth century is neither the end of history nor its beginning, but represents a new phase in that process which began two centuries ago with the accelerated progress of science and its application to production, the global expansion of industrial capitalism, and the rise of political movements challenging the domination of particular classes, élites and nations. There has been a succession of 'industrial revolutions', the most recent – the computer-information-automation revolution – being characterized especially by the emergence of a specific type of knowledge-based society (all human societies are knowledge-based in some way) such as Marx, in one of the most illuminating sections of the *Grundrisse* (1857–8, pp. 704–9), foresaw almost one hundred and fifty years ago. Among the most important changes which the rapid advance of science and technology is now producing are a radical reassessment of the nature and social role of work, the possibility of expanding greatly the sphere of leisure time, and the growing need for a more deliberate collective organization and regulation of production, with precise social aims that would necessarily include confronting the huge problems of bridging the gulf separating rich and poor countries, and of harmonizing production with the conservation, and indeed restoration, of the natural environment. From one aspect it may seem that coping with these changes will enhance the role of political élites, but this is a limited and misleading view. Far more important for the future of human societies throughout the world is the active intervention of ever larger numbers of educated and responsible citizens who have increasing leisure to devote to the self-regulation of their forms of life, and an awareness of the broader context and repercussions of their actions. In this process social movements of many different kinds are likely to have a growing influence, encouraging the necessary dissolution of the mystique of political élites and at the same time undermining the real dominance of upper classes.

NOTES

1 For a discussion of Schumpeter's schema, and of the criticisms brought against it, see Bottomore (1992, chap. 5).
2 'Accumulate, accumulate! That is Moses and the prophets!' as Marx wrote in *Capital* (1867, vol. I, chap. 24, sect. 3). Schumpeter, much influenced by Marxist thought, also regarded capitalism as an essentially dynamic, innovating system, necessarily committed to perpetual growth and expansion.
3 This closely resembles the comment by de Tocqueville; see above, p. 28.
4 See above, p. 30 and the studies by Hegedüs (1976, chap. 7) and Konrád and Szelényi (1979, chap. 10). I have discussed these issues more fully in Bottomore (1991a, chap. 3).
5 For a succinct account of the different forms of liberal democratic theory and practice, see Holden (1988, chap. 2); and on participatory democracy, Pateman (1970).
6 There is a large literature on various kinds of self-management, which includes studies of the former Yugoslav system, the cooperative movement and 'communities of work', expositions of Guild Socialism, anarchism and some versions of Marxism which emphasized the role of workers' councils; but so far as I am aware there is no comprehensive work analysing

systematically the policies that were proposed and implemented, or the nature of the problems that were encountered. The *Concise Encyclopaedia of Participation and Co-Management* (1992) does, however, provide much valuable information and analysis relating to these questions.

7 See especially Dogan (1975) and Suleiman (1978), and the broader studies of classes and élites in Bottomore and Brym (1989).

8 For example, by Aron (1950, 1960).

9 A general assembly of several thousands, hundreds of thousands, or millions of people, as a sole and universal method of deciding policies, is manifestly unworkable. Even on a smaller scale it presents many problems, as was illustrated by the general assemblies popular among radical students in the 1960s, whose principal (beneficial) achievement was in fact to increase student representation on various university committees. Referenda, as another means of eliciting the direct expression of opinion on important issues, also raise difficult and well-known problems.

Bibliography

Note: The date of first publication is followed, in relevant cases, by the date of the edition or translation used, to which page references are made in the text. Publication details of works by Marx and Engels are not generally given, since there are various, easily accessible translations.

Abercrombie, N. and Urry, J. 1983 *Capital, Labour and the Middle Classes* (London: Allen & Unwin).

Albertoni, Ettore A. 1987 *Mosca and the Theory of Élitism* (Oxford: Blackwell).

Armstrong, J.A. 1959 *The Soviet Bureaucratic Élite: A Case Study of the Ukrainian Apparatus* (London: Stevens & Sons).

Aron, Raymond 1950 'Social structure and the ruling class' (Reprinted in Aron 1988).

Aron, Raymond 1957 *The Opium of the Intellectuals* (London: Secker & Warburg).

Aron, Raymond 1960 'Classe sociale, classe politique, classe dirigeante' (Translated in Aron 1988).

Aron, Raymond 1966 *Peace and War: A Theory of International Relations* (New York: Doubleday).

Aron, Raymond 1988 *Power, Modernity and Sociology* (Aldershot: Edward Elgar).

Baltzell, D. 1962 *An American Business Aristocracy* (New York: Collier Books).

Barry, B. 1970 *Sociologists, Economists and Democracy* (London: Collier-Macmillan).

Beetham, D. 1981 'Michels and his critics', *European Journal of Sociology*, 22, 1.

Bell, Clive 1928 *Civilization: An Essay* (London: Chatto & Windus).

Bendix, R. 1949 *Higher Civil Servants in American Society* (Boulder: University of Colorado Press).

Berle, A.A. and Means, G.C. 1933 *The Modern Corporation and Private Property* (New York: Macmillan).

Bloch, Marc 1939–40 (1961) *Feudal Society* (London: Routledge & Kegan Paul).

Bottomore, Tom 1952 'La mobilité sociale dans la haute administration française', *Cahiers Internationaux de Sociologie*, XIII.

Bottomore, Tom 1967 *Critics of Society* (London: Allen & Unwin).

Bottomore, Tom 1991a *Classes in Modern Society* (2nd edn. London: Harper Collins).

Bottomore, Tom (ed.) 1991b *A Dictionary of Marxist Thought* (2nd edn. Oxford: Blackwell).

Bottomore, Tom 1992 *Between Marginalism and Marxism: The Economic Sociology of J.A. Schumpeter* (Hemel Hempstead: Harvester Wheatsheaf).

Bottomore, Tom and Brym, Robert J. (eds) 1989 *The Capitalist Class: An International Study* (Hemel Hempstead: Harvester Wheatsheaf).

Brinton, C. 1957 *The Anatomy of Revolution* (Englewood Cliffs: Prentice-Hall).

Brym, R. 1980 *Intellectuals and Politics* (London: Allen & Unwin).

Burnham, James 1943 *The Machiavellians: Defenders of Freedom* (London: Putnam).

Concise Encyclopaedia of Participation and Co-Management (ed. G. Széll) 1992 (Berlin and New York: Walter de Gruyter).

Copeman, G.H. 1955 *Leaders of British Industry: A Study of the Careers of More than a Thousand Public Company Directors* (London: Gee & Co.).

Croce, Benedetto 1913 *Historical Materialism and the Economics of Karl Marx* (London: Howard Latimer).

De Huszar, G.B. (ed.) 1960 *The Intellectuals: A Controversial Portrait* (Glencoe: Free Press).

Dent, J. 1973 *Crisis in Finance: Crown, Financiers and Society in Seventeenth Century France* (Newton Abbot: David & Charles).

Djilas, Milovan 1957 *The New Class* (London: Thames & Hudson).

Dogan, M. 1961 'Political ascent in a class society: French Deputies 1870–1958', in Marvick 1961.

Dogan, M. (ed.) 1975 *The Mandarins of Western Europe: The Political Role of Top Civil Servants* (London: Sage).

Downs, A. 1957 *An Economic Theory of Democracy* (New York: Harper).

Dreitzel, H.P. 1962 *Elitebegriff und Sozialstruktur* (Stuttgart: Ferdinand Enke).

Eliot, T.S. 1948 *Notes Towards the Definition of Culture* (London: Faber & Faber).

Field, F. (ed.) 1983 *The Wealth Report 2* (London: Routledge & Kegan Paul).

Finer, S.E. 1962 *The Man on Horseback: The Role of the Military in Politics* (London: Pall Mall Press).

Florence, P. Sargant 1953 *The Logic of British and American Industry* (London: Routledge & Kegan Paul).

Friedmann, Georges 1956 *The Anatomy of Work* (London: Heinemann).

Friedrich, C.J. 1950 *The New Image of the Common Man* (Boston: Beacon Press).

Gerth, H.H. and Mills, C. Wright (eds) 1947 *From Max Weber: Essays in Sociology* (London: Kegan Paul).

Ginsberg, M. 1936 (1947) 'The sociology of Pareto', in *Reason and Unreason in Society* (London: Longmans, Green).

Girard, Alain (ed.) 1961 *La réussite sociale en France: ses caractères, ses lois, ses effets* (Paris: Presses Universitaires de France).

Gramsci, Antonio 1964a 'La classe politica', in *Quaderni del Carcere*, vol. 4 (Milan: Einaudi).

Gramsci, Antonio 1964b 'Per una storia degli intellettuali', in *Quaderni del Carcere*, vol. 2 (Milan: Einaudi).

Guttsman, W.L. 1963 *The British Political Élite* (London: MacGibbon & Kee).

Hancock, G. 1991 *Lords of Poverty* (London: Mandarin Paperbacks).

Heath, A. 1981 *Social Mobility* (London: Fontana).

Hegedüs, Andras 1976 *Socialism and Bureaucracy* (London: Allison & Busby).

Hodgkin, T. 1961 *African Political Parties: An Introductory Guide* (Harmondsworth: Penguin Books).

Holden, B. 1988 *Understanding Liberal Democracy* (London: Philip Allan).

Jacobs, P. and Landau, S. (eds) 1966 *The New Radicals: A Report With Documents* (New York: Random House).

Jaher, F.C. (ed.) 1973 *The Rich, the Well Born and the Powerful* (Urbana: University of Illinois Press).

Janowitz, M. 1964 *The Military in the Political Development of New Nations* (Chicago: University of Chicago Press).

Kay, C. 1991 'Marxism in Latin America', in Bottomore 1991b.

Kelsall, R.K. 1955 *Higher Civil Servants in Britain* (London: Routledge & Kegan Paul).

Kerr, Clark, Dunlop, John T., Harbison, Frederick H. and Myers, Charles A. 1960 *Industrialism and Industrial Man* (Cambridge, Mass.: Harvard University Press).

Kingsley, J.D. 1944 *Representative Bureaucracy* (Yellow Springs: Antioch Press).

Kolabinska, Marie 1912 *La circulation des élites en France: Étude historique depuis la fin du XIe. siècle jusqu'à la Grande Révolution* (Lausanne: Imprimeries Réunies).

Konrád, G. and Szelényi, I. 1979 *The Intellectuals on the Road to Class Power* (Brighton: Harvester).

Lasswell, H.D., Lerner, D. and Rothwell, C.E. 1952 *The Comparative Study of Élites* (Stanford: Hoover Institute).

Le Goff, J. 1957 *Les intellectuels au Moyen Age* (Paris: Éditions du Seuil).

Lieuwen, E. 1961 *Arms and Politics in Latin America* (New York: Praeger).

Lukács, G. 1954 (1974) *The Destruction of Reason* (London: Merlin Press).

Lüthy, H. 1955 *The State of France* (London: Secker & Warburg).

Machajski, Waclaw 1905 *The Intellectual Worker* (Summarized in Nomad 1932).

McHugh, F. 1991 'Liberation theology', in Bottomore 1991b.

Maddison, A. 1982 *Phases of Capitalist Development* (Oxford: Oxford University Press).

Mannheim, Karl 1936 *Ideology and Utopia* (London: Kegan Paul).

Mannheim, Karl 1940 *Man and Society in an Age of Reconstruction* (London: Kegan Paul).

Mannheim, Karl 1956 *Essays on the Sociology of Culture* (London: Routledge & Kegan Paul).

Marsh, R.M. 1961 *The Mandarins: The Circulation of Élites in China, 1600–1900* (Glencoe: Free Press).

Marshall, Alfred 1873 (1925) 'The future of the working classes' (Reprinted in A.C. Pigou (ed.), *Memorials of Alfred Marshall*. London: Macmillan).

Marshall, G. 1982 *In Search of the Spirit of Capitalism: An Essay on Max Weber's Protestant Ethic Thesis* (London: Hutchinson).

Marshall, T.H. 1950 *Citizenship and Social Class* (Cambridge: Cambridge University Press).

Marshall, T.H. and Bottomore, Tom 1992 *Citizenship and Social Class* (London: Pluto Press).

Marvick, D. (ed.) 1961 *Political Decision-Makers* (Glencoe: Free Press).

Marx, Karl 1844 *Economic and Philosophical Manuscripts*.

Marx, Karl 1852 'The Chartists', *New York Daily Tribune*, 25 August.

Marx, Karl 1857–8 (1973) *Grundrisse* (Harmondsworth: Penguin Books).

Marx, Karl 1861–3 (1905–10) *Theories of Surplus Value* (3 vols ed. Karl Kautsky. Stuttgart, J.H.W. Dietz Nachf.)

Marx, Karl 1867, 1885, 1894 *Capital* (vols I, II and III).

Marx, Karl 1871 *The Civil War in France*.

Marx, Karl 1875 (1891) *Critique of the Gotha Programme*.

Marx, Karl and Engels, Friedrich 1845–6 (1932) *German Ideology*.

Meisel, J.H. 1958 *The Myth of the Ruling Class: Gaetano Mosca and the Élite* (Ann Arbor: University of Michigan Press).

Mercier, P. 1956 'Evolution of Senegalese élites', *International Social Science Bulletin*, VIII, 3.

Michels, R. 1911 (1966) *Political Parties* (New York: Free Press).

Miller, S.M. 1960 'Comparative social mobility', *Current Sociology*, IX, 1.

Miller, William (ed.) 1962 *Men in Business: Essays on the Historical Role of the Entrepreneur* (New York: Harper & Row).

Mills, C. Wright 1956 *The Power Élite* (New York: Oxford University Press).

Misra, B.B. 1961 *The Indian Middle Classes* (London: Oxford University Press).

Mosca, Gaetano 1884 *Sulla Teorica dei governi e sul governo parlamentare: Studi storici e sociali* (Turin: Loescher).

Mosca, Gaetano 1896 *Elementi di scienza politica* (2nd revised and enlarged edn 1923. English version conflating the two editions in Mosca 1939).

Mosca, Gaetano 1937 *Storia delle dottrine politiche* (Bari: Laterza).

Mosca, Gaetano 1939 *The Ruling Class* (New York: McGraw-Hill).

Nadel, S.F. 1956 'The concept of social élites', *International Social Science Bulletin*, VIII, 3.

Nomad, Max 1932 *Rebels and Renegades* (New York: Macmillan).

Ortega y Gasset, J. 1930 (1961) *The Revolt of the Masses* (London: Allen & Unwin).

Ossowski, S. 1963 *Class Structure in the Social Consciousness* (London: Routledge & Kegan Paul).

Pareto, Vilfredo 1896–7 *Cours d'économie politique* (Lausanne: Librairie de l'Université).

Pareto, Vilfredo 1902 *Les systèmes socialistes* (2 vols. Paris: Marcel Giard).

Pareto, Vilfredo 1915–19 (1963) *A Treatise on General Sociology* (New York: Dover).

Pateman, C. 1970 *Participation and Democratic Theory* (Cambridge: Cambridge University Press).

Pirenne, H. 1914 'Periods in the social history of capitalism', *American Historical Review*, April.

Playford, C. and Pond, C. 1983 'The right to be unequal: inequality in incomes', in Field 1983.

Pond, C. 1983 'Wealth and the two nations', in Field 1983.

Pye, L.W. 1961 'Armies in the process of political modernization', *European Journal of Sociology*, II, 1.

Rousseau, Jean-Jacques 1755 (1913) *A Dissertation on the Origin and Foundation of the Inequality of Mankind* (In the Everyman Library edn of *The Social Contract and Discourses*. London: Dent).

Sampson, A. 1962 *Anatomy of Britain* (London: Hodder & Stoughton).

Schumpeter, J.A. 1927 (1951) 'Social classes in an ethnically homogeneous environment' (In English in Paul M. Sweezy (ed.), *Imperialism and Social Classes*. Oxford: Blackwell).

Schumpeter, J.A. 1939 *Business Cycles: A Theoretical, Historical and Statistical Analysis of the Capitalist Process* (New York: McGraw-Hill).

Schumpeter, J.A. 1942 (1987) *Capitalism, Socialism and Democracy* (London: Allen & Unwin).

Scott, John 1979 *Corporations, Classes and Capitalism* (London: Hutchinson).

Scott, John 1982 *The Upper Classes: Property and Privilege in Britain* (London: Macmillan).

Scott, John 1991 *Who Rules Britain?* (Oxford: Blackwell/Polity).

Sereno, Renzo 1938 'The anti-Aristotelianism of Gaetano Mosca and its fate', *Ethics*, XLVIII, 4.

Siegfried, André 1957 *De la IIIème à la IVème République* (Paris: Grasset).

Skocpol, T. 1979 *States and Social Revolutions* (Cambridge: Cambridge University Press).

Smythe, H.H. and Smythe, M.M. 1960 *The New Nigerian Élite* (Stanford: Stanford University Press).

Steward, J.H. (ed.) 1955 *Irrigation Civilizations: A Comparative Study* (Pan-American Union).

Suleiman, E.N. 1978 *Élites in French Society* (Princeton: Princeton University Press).

Tawney, R.H. 1952 *Equality* (London: Allen & Unwin).

Titmuss, R. 1962 *Income Distribution and Social Change* (London: Allen & Unwin).

Toynbee, Arnold J. 1934–61 *A Study of History* (12 vols. London: Oxford University Press).

Van Niel, R. 1960 *The Emergence of the Modern Indonesian Élite* (The Hague: W. Van Hoeve).

Veblen, Thorstein 1921 *The Engineers and the Price System* (New York: Viking Press).

Weber, Max 1904 ' "Objectivity" in social science and social policy', in Weber 1949.

Weber, Max 1904–5 (1976) *The Protestant Ethic and the Spirit of Capitalism* (London: Allen & Unwin).

Weber, Max 1919 'Politics as a vocation', in Gerth and Mills 1947.

Weber, Max 1920 'The Chinese Literati', in Gerth and Mills 1947.

Weber, Max 1921 'Bureaucracy', in Weber 1921 (1968) and in Gerth and Mills 1947.

Weber, Max 1921 (1968) *Economy and Society* (New York: Bedminster Press).

Weber, Max 1923 (1961) *General Economic History* (New York: Collier Books).

Weber, Max 1949 *The Methodology of the Social Sciences* (New York: Free Press).

White, G., Murray, R. and White, C. (eds) 1983 *Revolutionary Socialist Development in the Third World* (Brighton: Wheatsheaf).

Williams, Raymond 1958 *Culture and Society* (Harmondsworth: Penguin Books).

Wittfogel, Karl 1957 *Oriental Despotism* (New Haven: Yale University Press).

Name index

Abercrombie, N. 62
Albertoni, E.A. 13, 122, 123, 128, 129
Armstrong, J.A. 71
Aron, R. 7, 56, 78, 90, 92, 99n; on classless society 107–8; on pluralistic democracy 89, 93, 97, 98

Baltzell, D. 61
Barry, B. 89
Bell, C. 114
Bendix, R. 71
Berle, A.A. 60
Bottomore, T. 21, 68, 130n
Boütmy, E. 68
Brinton, C. 49, 50
Brym, R. 21, 70
Burnham, J. 59, 60

Carlyle, T. 8, 11
Comte, A. 13
Copeman, G.H. 62
Croce, B. 33

Dent, J. 47
Djilas, M. 65, 66
Dogan, M. 57
Downs, A. 89
Dreitzel, H.P. 12

Eliot, T.S. 97, 100, 115

Finer, S.E. 85
Florence, P.S. 61
Friedmann, G. 100, 118
Friedrich, C.J. 8, 23, 69

Ginsberg, M. 51
Girard, A. 57, 70
Gramsci, A. 5
Guttsmann, W.L. 47, 99n

Hancock, G. 86
Heath, A. 47
Hodgkin, T. 77

Jacobs, B. 119
Jaher, F.C. 47
Janowitz, M. 85

Kay, C. 80
Kelsall, R.K. 68
Kerr, C. 74, 77
Kingsley, J.D. 32
Kolabinska, M. 4, 10, 36, 39–40, 46, 51

Landau, S. 119
Lasswell, H.D. 6, 13, 54
Le Goff, J. 54
Lieuwen, E. 82, 85
Lincoln, A. 90

Lukács, G. 8
Lüthy, H. 67

Machajski, W. 54
McHugh, F. 80
Maddison, A. 122
Mannheim, K. 31, 54, 55, 90, 93, 94;
  on élites in democracy 9, 87–8,
  97, 100
Marsh, R.M. 47, 53
Marshall, A. 113
Marshall, T.H. 123
Marvick, D. 47
Marx, K. 21, 22, 42, 48, 60, 63, 95,
  117n, 129; and a classless society
  103–7, 111; criticism of 17, 18;
  revolutionary theory of 49, 50;
  social theory of 15–16, 20; on
  universal suffrage 32
Means, G.C. 60
Meisel, J.H. 4, 10, 13, 22, 42
Michels, R. 10, 14, 87, 90, 94, 107
Miller, S.M. 46, 51
Miller, W. 46, 47, 61
Mills, C.W. 61, 69, 71, 108; on
  power élite 22, 23, 24, 25, 26
Misra, B.B. 75
Mosca, G. 2, 11, 13, 16, 70, 87, 122;
  on circulation of élites 6, 40–2,
  45, 46, 48; élite theory of 3, 4, 5,
  10, 13; and governing élite 22, 33,
  85n; on intellectuals 55; and
  social forces 22, 26, 49, 98

Nadel, S.F. 14
Nietzsche, F. 8, 11
Nomad, M. 54, 70

Ortega y Gasset 91, 114

Ossowski, S. 21, 66

Pareto, V. 5, 8, 10, 11, 16, 26, 49,
  51n, 70, 87; on circulation of
  élites 22, 33–9, 44–5, 48; élite
  theory of 1–2, 3, 4, 6, 13
Pirenne, H. 42, 43, 45, 46, 48, 51
Plato 13
Playford, C. 28
Pond, C. 28
Pye, L.W. 82

Rousseau, J.J. 102

Saint-Simon, C.H. 13
Sampson, A. 24
Schumpeter, J.A. 9, 11, 45, 46, 48,
  49, 70, 121, 130n; and democracy
  88–9, 93; on feudalism 17; on
  social classes 43–4
Scott, J. 32, 62
Siegfried, A. 67
Skocpol, T. 50
Smythe, H.H. 77

Titmuss, R. 33
Tocqueville, A. de 28, 91, 130
Toynbee, A. 115, 118

Urry, J. 62

Van Niel, R. 77
Veblen, T. 59

Weber, M. 8, 9, 10, 17, 27, 30, 32,
  42, 53; and bureaucracy 63–4; on
  capitalism 18
Williams, R. 9
Wittfogel, K. 29, 30

Subject index

Adam Smith Institute 57
Africa: middle class in 75; military in 82; nationalism in 80; political élites in 77–8; social structure in 73; socialism in 84
anti-élitism 127–8, 129
Arab States: dynastic élites in 75, 76, 83; middle class in 76; military in 83; nationalism in 81; social structure in 73
aristocracies 2, 4, 19, 35, 37
armies, political role of 82–3
Asia: middle class in 75; military in 82; nationalism in 80; social structure in 73; *see also* China; India
automation, effects of 112

Bill of Rights 126
bourgeoisie 19–20
bureaucratic élite 63–9, 70, 124; education for 68, 69
business élite 23, 24, 26, 52, 59–63, 70, 120; circulation of 46, 69; in developing countries 76; in UK 62, 63; in USA 61–2

capitalism 21, 60, 84, 121–2; and democracy 89; Marxist theory of 15–16, 18, 60, 106; Pirenne and 42–3; Veblen on 59; Weber and 18

charisma 8, 128
Charter 88, 126
Chile 76
China 84; *literati* in 29, 53
circulation of élites 6, 10, 31; comparisons of 48; in democracies 94, 97–8; in France 40; measurement of 46–8; military and 82–3; Mosca on 40–2; Pareto on 35–9, 44–5; and social class 43–4, 45, 49
citizenship 123, 129
civil service 20, 68, 69, 71
civilization, exceptional individuals in 114–15
class conflict 15–16, 26, 98
classless society 16, 21, 54, 109; Aron and 107–9, 111; Marx and 103–7, 111
collective ownership 110
colonial administrators 74–5
communism 61, 91; collapse of 120; in developing countries 78, 79; ruling groups and 30
Communist Party 65–6; in USSR 79, 124–5
company directors 60
competition for power 9, 87, 88, 89, 90, 93, 94, 98, 111
control: over the economy 125; over

élites 23, 24, 67–8
counter-élite 6, 8
creative minority 115, 118
creativity 115–16
Cuba 84
culture: changes in 49; in a classless
    society 116; Eliot on 115–16; and
    nationalism 81

decentralization of political authority
    108, 109, 111
democracy 29, 90–1, 101, 111, 129;
    in élite theories 4, 6, 8–9, 11, 89,
    97–8, 122–3; élites in 23–4, 87–8,
    89–90, 91–4; and equality 123;
    and society 95–7
determinism 11, 22
developing countries: economic
    development in 120–1; élites in
    72–85, 124; military regimes in
    124
dictatorship of the proletariat 107
direct action 9
distinction between rulers and ruled
    2, 3, 4, 6, 11, 21, 25, 90, 94, 116
division of labour 104–5, 111–13
dynastic élites 75, 83

Eastern Europe 30, 66, 84, 107;
    collapse of communism in 120;
    new élites in 120–1
economic depression 121
economic development: and élite
    circulation 43; middle class and
    75, 76–7; nationalism and 81;
    political élite and 77–8, 80
economic élite see business élite
economic enterprises, self-
    government in 110, 112, 130n
economic growth 121, 122
education: for bureaucratic élite 68,
    69; expansion in 113; and
    ideology of élite 96–7
electoral reform 126; resistance to 128

élites: circulation of see circulation of
    élites; in a civilized society
    114–15; in a classless society
    107–8; composition of 3, 4;
    definition of 1–2, 12–13; in
    democracy 23–4, 87–8, 89–90,
    91–4; psychological characteristics
    of 37, 38, 41; recruitment to see
    recruitment to élite; role of in
    economic and social development
    120–30; and social class 123; and
    socialism 10, 11, 15; and
    sub-élites 5; unification of 107,
    108; see also bureaucratic élite;
    business élite; intellectual élite;
    military élite; political élite
engineers 59, 60
entrepreneurs 76, 77, 83, 89
environment, damage to 119, 120
equality 101–3, 111, 128; and élite
    theory 103–17; of opportunity 9,
    10, 117; see also inequality
European Community 127

Fabians 57
Fascism 61, 87, 91
feudalism 17, 19, 21
France: bureaucratic élite in 67, 68,
    69; élites in 36, 40; intellectual
    élite in 54, 56–7, 58
functional élites 7, 123–4

game theory 99n
Germany: bureaucracy in 64;
    democracy in 97; NSP in 124;
    warrior nobility in 44
Ghana 77
governing élite see political élite;
    ruling élite
government officials, in developing
    countries 76–7

homogeneity, of social origins of élite
    23, 97

human actions, and residues 37

ideal type concept 27, 33
ideology: and élites 10, 12, 96–7; and
    social change 18–19, 60
independence struggles 73, 80, 81
India 81, 91; Brahmins in 29, 53–4;
    élite in 39; Marxism in 79–80;
    middle class in 75; nationalist
    leaders in 78
individuals: circulation of 35, 45, 48,
    94, 97; self-determination for
    103–4; social life of 106
Indonesia 77
industrial revolutions 129
industrialization: of developing
    countries 73, 74; and élites 74–7;
    Marxism and 79; *see also*
    economic development
industry, separation of ownership and
    control of 60, 61, 125
inequality 96, 97, 102, 122–3; of
    nations 119; and social class 104;
    see also equality
intellectual élite 5, 7, 29, 52, 53–9;
    composition of 56, 58; political
    attitudes of 57–8; social prestige
    of 56–7
intellectuals 53–7, 69, 70, 124; and
    independence movements 77–8,
    79
intelligentsia 53, 75
interests 26; élites and 6, 36, 42, 48,
    70; of intellectuals 56
International Monetary Fund 84, 119

labour movements, role of
    intellectual élite in 54, 55–6
laissez-faire 9, 10
land, ownership of 28, 30
landowners 17, 18, 29, 30
Latin America: dynastic élites in 75,
    83; Marxism in 80; middle class
    in 76; nationalism in 81; new

élites in 76; social structure in 73
leadership 50, 88, 128; in developing
    countries 74, 80–1; nationalist
    77–8, 80, 83
Left Book Club 57
leisure class 112

managerial revolution 59–60, 63, 67
Marxism 10, 11, 19, 26, 52; and
    independence movements 78,
    79–80
mass society 2–3, 4, 25, 108–9; and
    democracy 88, 91, 94
means of production, ownership of
    30, 65, 125
measurement, of élite circulation 46–7
media events, to promote élites 128
middle classes 21, 32; in developing
    countries 75–7, 83; new 5, 6, 53
military élite 17, 19, 23, 24, 25, 26; in
    developing countries 81–3, 124;
    in France 40
multinational corporations 21, 60,
    109, 119, 120

nationalism 80–1
nationalist leaders 77–8, 80, 83
neo-élitism 128–9
new élites: in developing countries
    72, 74, 76; formation of 35, 36,
    41, 44, 50; military and 82–3
Nicaragua 76
Nigeria 77

on-party states 79, 91, 92–3, 124–5

Paris Commune 104
participatory democracy 125, 126–7,
    129
political change 22, 44, 45; and
    circulation of élite 46
political class 5, 7–8
political élite 3, 5, 6, 21–2, 69, 123,
    124–6, 130; cohesion of 25, 26,

97; in a democracy 96; in developing countries 77–8; disillusionment with 128; extent of 7–8; and non-élite 2, 4; Pareto on 2, 23, 35, 36, 37, 39; sub-groups of 41; *see also* ruling class

political instability 74

political parties 88, 89, 92, 93, 94–5, 125; centralization of power in 128

political power 3, 6–7, 22, 107–8, 124, 125; in capitalist society 20, 21; in a democracy 90, 91; in developing countries 83; and military 81–2; and the ruling class 19; of the upper class 27

'Port Huron Statement' 119

power: centralization of 128; economic 19, 21, 29, 60, 107–8, 109–10; and the ruling class 19, 20, 21; *see also* political power; political élite

power élite 30, 124, 125; Mills on 22, 23, 25, 26

pressure groups 126

Protestant ethic 18

psychological characteristics of élite 37, 38, 41

public ownership 21, 111, 112

public schools 20

qualities of élite 41–2

recruitment to élite 5, 6, 7, 39, 41, 44, 46, 52, 61; and the civil service 68, 71; in democracies 87, 94, 98

Reform Act (1832) 20

representative government 4, 90, 91, 125, 129

residues 6, 37–8

revolutions 49–50, 60; and élite circulation 36, 37, 39, 48; role of intellectual élite in 54, 55

ruling class 25–6, 27, 85; composition of 30–1; and élite

circulation 41, 42; ideal type of 27–8; in Marxist theory 10, 15, 19, 20–1; and ownership of property 29, 30; as power élite 22–5, 26–7; *see also* political élite

scientists 58, 60

self-government 99

Senegal 85

service class 63

social change 17, 19; and élite circulation 44–6; and élites in developing countries 72

social class 10, 66, 70, 97, 98; and élite circulation 43–4, 45, 49; and élites 124–5; and inequality 104; of intellectuals 56, 58; sub-groups of 49

social democracy 97

social élite 114–15

social equilibrium 37; and new élites 35–6, 44

social forces 4, 6, 22, 26, 49, 98

social groups, rise and fall of 45, 49, 50–1

social life, commercialization of 120

social mobility *see* circulation of élites

social movements 126, 128, 130

social structures 17; changes in 21, 44, 45, 49; and élites in developing countries 72

socialism 123; in developing countries 79–80, 84; élite theories and 10–11, 15; intellectual élite and 54–5, 56

Soviet Marxism 79

state, control of over economic production 21, 109, 122

sub-élites 5, 6, 49, 70

subject classes 15, 21, 26

summit meetings 128

superiority 10

taxation 28

technology 129, 130; changes in 45
Third World *see* developing countries
trade union élite 36
traditional élites, in developing
    countries 81, 83

United Kingdom: company directors
    in 62, 63; democracy in 126–7;
    distribution of wealth in 28;
    intellectuals in 57; recruitment to
    civil service in 68
United States of America 47; chief
    executives in 61–2; and
    counter-revolutions in Latin
    America 76; mass society in
    108–9; power élites in 23, 25
unity of the élite 23, 97–8
universal suffrage 20–1, 31, 32, 125
universities 110; intellectual élite and
    54, 56
upper class 2, 27, 28, 94, 98; culture
    and 115, 116; as élites 23, 117,
    128; officials from 68; and

ownership of property 28
USSR: bureaucracy in 71; classless
    society in 107–8; élites in 65, 66,
    89; Marxism in 19, 79; one-party
    state in 124–5
Utilitarians 18, 57

voluntary associations 98, 99; culture
    and 116; importance of 109, 110

wealth: inequalities of 119;
    ownership of 27, 28, 62, 63; and
    participation in government 96
welfare state 21
work: changes in 112, 113; nature of
    130
working class 52, 113–14; Marx on
    16, 20, 21
World Bank 84, 119

Yugoslavia 99, 130n

Zimbabwe 84